Leveraging People for a Corporate Turnaround

Leadership and Management Guidance

for Organizational Change

Yuval Bar-Or, Ph.D.

TLB Publishing

Springfield, New Jersey

www.TLBcorp.com

Human pyramid on cover © iStockphoto.com/Dan Tero

Library of Congress Cataloging-in-Publication Data

Bar-Or, Yuval, 1967–

Leveraging People for a Corporate Turnaround: Leadership and Management Guidance for Organizational Change / Yuval Bar-Or

p.   cm.

Includes bibliographical references and index.

ISBN 13: 978-0-9800118-3-8

ISBN 10: 0-9800118-3-3

1. Business. 2. Leadership. 3. Management. 4. Corporate Turnaround. 5. Organizational Change. I. Title.

Printed in the United States of America

In memory of Oded Bar-Or

Acknowledgements

My thanks to Kate Steele of The Editorial Department, whose expertise, energy and attention to detail played a substantial role in transforming a rough manuscript into a real book. I also thank Marilyn Bar-Or and Tali Rich for their early comments and feedback, and Ralph Samson for technical and design assistance.

Table of Contents

There is nothing more difficult to take in hand, more perilous to conduct, or more uncertain in its success, than to take the lead in the introduction of a new order of things. Because the innovator has for enemies all those who have done well under the old conditions and only lukewarm defenders in those who may do well under the new.

Niccolo Machiavelli, *The Prince*

INTRODUCTION

This book recounts the thought processes and the actions necessary to turn an ailing company or business unit around.

Much of the significant body of literature on corporate turnarounds focuses on business operations: legal, bankruptcy, and management accounting issues. Too often, when staff is considered, they are merely an expense to be cut, a commodity to "downsize" or "rightsize": regardless of how it's labeled, it still means *firing people*. The most mean-spirited among those books and articles can be summarized as "how to fire employees without paying them severance."

My purpose is to share my own business turnaround knowledge and experience, combining current management and operations Best Practices with the most practical, easily grasped principles and processes for leveraging people's diverse talents and skills, in order to stanch the red ink, heal the wounds in the corporate body, and put the company back on its feet.

This book is written for:

- Executives entrusted with the authority and responsibility for a turnaround;

- Leaders, executives and managers in growing companies;

- Entrepreneurs planning new ventures;

- Managers in companies that have stopped growing, or must change dramatically to survive;

- Executives and officers in military, government, service organizations, or any other human endeavor requiring leadership to survive, change, and thrive.

- Individuals contemplating career choices or changes, seeking guidance in evaluating business organizations to see if they "fit."

The book proceeds from here with 11 chapters, grouped into five parts. Part One explores people-specific issues and momentum, Part Two outlines the process of assessing the firm's current state, Part Three aims at pinpointing the causes of the firm's dysfunction, Part Four outlines actions necessary to effect the turnaround, and Part Five provides guidance once the turnaround takes hold.

PART ONE
PEOPLE and MOMENTUM

Chapter 1

People are Key to Every Turnaround

The expression "People are our greatest asset" has been uttered by many CEOs (some even genuinely mean it). There is, however, the generally unspoken corollary to this cliché: "People are our greatest liability."

One need not look further than the evening news to find examples. The most damaging human "liabilities" are powerful executives and key personnel: high profile cases of their criminal behavior at large corporations—Enron and WorldCom, among others—come to mind.

Anyone who has spent any time in business, family, or other social settings knows that some individuals are very predictable: dependably optimistic individuals, who lift our spirits with a smile, know just the right words to say; or those dependably grouchy pessimists who may be the very cause of our need for a dose of optimism. Deciding which are "assets" and which are "liabilities" is not difficult.

The vast majority of us, however, are not so clear in our behavioral choices, not so immune to our circumstances and surroundings. One individual can begin a job optimistic, enthusiastic, committed to the team and company—and end employment discouraged, disappointed, at the extreme, feeling angry and betrayed, desiring to "get even" with the company. A true asset has become a liability.

The firm suffers significantly, whether asset-turned-liability people actively sabotage the company by stealing money or merely sapping efficiency and morale with their negative attitudes and behavior.

Why do human assets become human liabilities? How does that happen? Can companies protect themselves against such losses?

One of this book's main themes is that the most elemental difference between successful and failing companies is how well people function separately, and together as groups, teams, business units and corporations.

People's skills, concerns, motives, aspirations, and deficiencies are a central factor in determining success for an enterprise. This chapter addresses five elements to consider in creating—or re-inventing—the functional and support infrastructures necessary to every company, regardless of size:

- The Significance of Emotional Intelligence;

- The Meaning of "Leader" and "Manager;"

- The Key Drivers of Human Behavior;

- The "Top Twelve" Constructive Human Traits;

- The "Dirty Dozen" Destructive Human Traits.

As you embark on a turnaround effort, begin by observing people you encounter, noticing how they walk, stand or sit; their facial expressions and gestures; is the general style of their clothing flamboyant, conservative, or somewhere between? Be very aware of your own reactions to what you see and hear: are your biases and prejudices preventing you from being open-minded and perceiving others accurately? Observing how your staff, clients, suppliers, and partners perform in the course of your day-to-day contacts with them is clearly necessary if you are to understand how best to run your company.

Do not shrink from scrutinizing your Board, your boss(es)—and yourself—as honestly as the competition does.

Emotional Intelligence

Let's begin by reviewing some terminology.

"Intelligence" is the *capacity or potential* for learning.

Cognitive (intellectual) *capacity* pertains to the mental processes of perception, memory, judgment, and reasoning. These are summarized by the traditional IQ measurement.

Emotional intelligence is the *capacity* for self-awareness, motivation, self-regulation, empathy, and adeptness in relationships; in order to distinguish it from IQ, Emotional Intelligence is often referred to as EQ.

Cognitive skills (IQ), emotional skills (EQ), and experience are synergistic; competence—the combination of traits, habits, expertise that sets high achievers apart from less stellar performers—requires mastery of *both* cognitive and emotional capacities.

The key thesis is that *emotional intelligence is more critical to professional and personal success than intellect, education, or technical skill.* The higher you intend to rise in business, the more critical emotional competencies become. Consider a quote in Daniel Goleman's seminal book, *Emotional Intelligence: Why It Can Matter More Than IQ.* The quote is attributed to a head of research at a global executive search firm:

"CEOs are hired for their intellect and business expertise—and fired for a lack of emotional intelligence."

Lack of emotional competencies is particularly damaging in a turnaround situation because human fallibilities are magnified a hundred-fold in a distressed firm. Stress, distrust, paranoia, and lack of confidence are at all-time highs in troubled firms. People need to feel their fears and concerns are being heard; empathetic responses, coupled with straightforward answers, usually calm fears long enough for people to think rationally. Understanding their emotional needs is critical to motivating and redirecting them to the common cause: a cold shoulder, denial or denigration of human emotions, or disrespect by a leader can cause anxiety to increase exponentially.

Awareness of how emotions affect performance is the primary emotional competence: our emotions affect us, and the people around us; their emotions affect them, and the people around them.

This point bears repeating: the primary emotional competence is awareness of how emotions affect performance.

In order to move the company forward, it is absolutely necessary for you, the leader, to be emotionally competent. If you do not understand how to manage yourself, or how to model for others the meshing of self-mastery with technical expertise and experience, you have no chance to motivate your staff or enable them to work together more constructively—especially during those moments when anxiety is peaking.

Anxious people do not think clearly; uncontrolled emotions take up so much short-term memory, the capacity for rational thought and behavior is limited.

Businessmen who were tough (read "abusive") to their staff used to be considered "shrewd." Anyone who cared about employees' emotions and concerns was considered "too soft" for management and faced a "glass (or concrete) ceiling" or escort to the exit door.

In recent decades these fallacies have been exposed for what they are: false notions based on incomplete data and mechanistic behavioral models. Fortunately, modern studies of human behavior demonstrate clearly that recognizing others' humanity is critical to increasing productivity, not a sign of weakness. Multiple studies show unequivocally that employees who are happy tend to stay in one place longer, and are more productive.

Thus, the concept of emotional competence is no longer seen as "softness" but accepted by academic and business mainstreams as a highly desired skill a leader and manager must possess to succeed.

This book is not suggesting that you buy the proverbial black leather couch and become a therapist to your staff, but it does suggest that emotional competence is a *minimum qualification* for any management or leadership position. Effective management elicits the best performance from people by understanding their needs and aspirations. Some people may respond well to deadline pressures and thrive on stress, while others need peace and quiet to do their best work. Most respond to some combination of both, and the same person may be more responsive to deadlines one day, but need to retreat from office bustle the next.

Developing emotional competence is a *learning* process; anyone who possesses the native emotional intelligence and awareness that emotions can enhance or destroy one's ability to think can become emotionally competent.

Demonstrating your own emotional competence and requiring your senior managers to follow your lead to invigorate individual and collective performance is intrinsic to your turnaround goals.

Bear in mind that a leader is also human and subject to the same emotions, concerns, yearnings, and ambitions that affect everyone else in the group. The big difference: you, as the leader, *must* exhibit greater self-control and take greater care in what you say publicly, and make certain that your tone and demeanor consistently reinforce your positive messages.

Just as these principles of emotional competence apply to you and your staff, they apply to everyone else connected with your firm, including partners and clients. Clearly, clients who've suffered due to the ailing firm's dysfunction will need your undivided attention to "hear" their complaints and discern how best to make amends. Slighted partners may have a similar need to feel their anger and disappointment is being heard.

Leadership and Management

"Leadership" and "management," or "leader" and "manager," are often used interchangeably; this section strives to differentiate between the two in subsequent discussions of critical knowledge and skills needed to achieve the turnaround:

- "Leadership" has to do with the ability to inspire others and gain their trust; to convey a strategic vision other people will voluntarily support. Leadership is about changing mindsets, convincing people of the need to effect change; establishing why your vision is correct, or why it may be more correct than a current path.

- "Management" pertains to the ability to direct people to combine their diverse experiences and talents in the most effective way to produce desired results. It requires emotional competencies to identify abilities and skill deficiencies in others, and determine how to combine people within a team to optimize performance.

Leadership is more inspirational in nature; management's focus is more operational; these abbreviated definitions suffice here.

The distinctions between these two are critical to the turnaround, or for that matter, to any situation in which change is required.

Recognize that not everyone aspires to management or leadership, or is suited for these roles. Technical genius—whether in accounting, the lab, or on the shop floor—is its own reward to those who possess it. True leaders and managers protect technicians by establishing "dual career tracks," one for technicians, one for leaders.

As you evaluate organizational performance, ascertain which managers, most senior to most junior, possess the necessary emotional competency to move up in the firm as they are, and which ones need to develop their emotional intelligence as part of their professional development plan.

Asking yourself how many leadership attributes you possess, and how many managerial skills you possess requires rigorous honesty. Do you possess enough of both to succeed in the assignment you have accepted?

Nine emotional competencies are most commonly associated with successful executives:

- The drive to achieve, the ability to work wholeheartedly toward a goal;

- Readiness and ability to take the initiative for responsible decisions; and

- The ability to adapt, let go of old assumptions and accept change positively.

- The ability to influence or persuade others, to *sell* ideas;

- The ability to inspire and guide others in pursuing collective goals, cultivating opportunities through people with complementary skills and aspirations;

- The ability to comprehend emotional currents and counter-currents and discern who wields power, official and unofficial, and influence in an organization.

- The ability to "read' others' feelings, needs, and concerns and refuse to exploit them for personal gain;

- The honesty to recognize and "own" our individual strengths and weaknesses, value, trust, and use our own talents and intuition;

- The ability to discern others' capacities and desire to improve their technical and social skills, and evaluate their performance fairly, without bias or prejudice.

Intuition is a somewhat misunderstood concept, deserving of clarification. While often viewed as a magical capability, intuition is widely believed in scientific circles to be nothing other than pattern recognition. As we observe an event, and contemplate an appropriate response, our brain seeks similar past experiences and signals such matches or near-matches through our nervous system. One of the neurological pathways carrying the news of a match is believed to travel to the abdominal region, explaining why we often think of intuition as a 'gut feeling.' In fact, intuition is very much a neurobiological process of comparison to an existing store of experiences. Intuition development therefore begins with exposure to a breadth of experiences.

For simplicity in subsequent chapters, the words "leader" and "manager" may be used interchangeably to refer to the person with the top decision-making authority. Context should be your guide in deciding which particular skill set is being discussed, if such a distinction appears important.

Key Drivers of Human Behavior

Fundamental priorities, or needs, drive the behavior of all people; some psychologists refer to them as "emotional imperatives." Depending on circumstances and personal priorities, individuals may rank their personal drivers differently, but the same emotional imperatives are common across cultures. Emotional states are complex and rarely pure: mixtures of anger, sorrow, apprehension, and self-doubt can underlie an individual's or group's behavior. For example, an individual may experience being constrained by a glass ceiling as being denied control over her own advancement, injury to her personal dignity, and unfair treatment, all at one time.

Compensation: Most people have to work to make a living; the hard currency they bring home is of utmost importance—it literally does put food on the table. People are happiest and most motivated when they feel their efforts are justly rewarded. Conversely, people resent being underpaid. The resentment will affect their motivation, morale, demeanor and longevity the workplace.

Compensation stability is a matter of black letter and case law, not to mention the revised codes of legislative bodies. Most people rely upon the predictability of their paychecks to make important life decisions such as having a child or borrowing to buy a house, or car, or boat. Setting money aside in children's college funds and committing funds to retirement savings accounts also require predictable income.

Money is not the only "compensation" work generates: most people are strongly attracted to work that is satisfying and meaningful, using their energies, skills and talents to their highest and best purpose. "Good work" enhances life.

Work in distressed companies is typically less than "good work"; employers who cause "paycheck anxiety" break trust with their employees. Once this fundamental trust is broken, loyalties erode; staff are less willing to "go the extra mile" in hard times. Employees with valuable talent and institutional knowledge are likely to be most disappointed, offended, or resentful; the company is at risk for losing momentum and market-share if their best people choose to leave.

If paychecks are consistently late, incorrect, or employees believe they have been shortchanged, not only will you lose their services, you may have regulatory agencies investigating their complaints to add to your already long list of turnaround problems.

Upward Mobility, Sense of Personal Direction and Satisfaction: Very few people see any point in a job with no future: most desire to advance in their careers. They take great pride in moving up in the ranks, earning a greater share of responsibility in the firm, gaining increasing respect among their peers, and reaping the financial rewards and personal satisfaction of advancement.

When that sense of direction or upward trajectory is in danger or completely disappears, personal motivation will waver as concern about future prospects grows: commitment wavers when you feel that regardless of the effort you put in, the rewards you were led to reasonably expect won't be forthcoming.

The glass ceiling is a major culprit in this category of human need. Imagine the frustration of working hard, often for years—proving yourself every step of the way—only to be blocked by some invisible barrier. The barrier is not physically visible and cannot be touched, but over time, it's clear that it exists and isn't going away. The longer the barriers to satisfaction last, the more likely employees will finally "have enough" and depart.

Troubled firms will also be in desperate need of leaders, both in the short- and long-term. In the short-term, there will be a need for leaders at all levels who can rally people to a cause while all hell seems to be breaking loose around them. In the longer-term, once you've developed traction and some positive momentum, you will need leaders at all levels to support and sustain the firm's growth.

Failure to develop individuals, or to promote them to leadership roles when they are ready, is a recipe for disaster.

Example: *I knew a manager who expanded his consulting practice aggressively. His unit grew from 4 people to 19 in less than a year. By the end of that period, he had each and every one of these 19 people reporting to him directly. I asked him why* *he hadn't promoted a couple of them to intermediate leadership positions, with more junior staff reporting to them in a pyramidal reporting structure. His answer was that none of them were worthy of a leadership position.*

The manager became predictably over-extended with people-management duties, and was unable to spend sufficient time with any one person. He was also unable to properly attend to all his other duties. Eventually, his staff deserted in large numbers. It was hard to believe, that across that pool of talent, not a single person manifested sufficient skills to be rewarded and challenged with greater responsibility. This appeared to be a classic example of either failure to develop people properly or failure to entrust them with increasing responsibilities when they were ready for the challenge.

Over time, I came to conclude that the issues were more complex than an inability to recognize the talents of others, or an inclination to micromanage. Rather, it turned out that the manager in question had some concerns his boss was seeking to replace him, and he feared that by empowering and advancing someone else, he might be laying the groundwork for his own dismissal.

This exposed yet another layer of emotional incompetence. There was lack of confidence and very poor communication between the two managers, and the uncertainty this created led to undeserved retaliatory action against junior personnel.

Clarity, Sense of Corporate Direction: Basic belief that their jobs are "safe" in the near-term, and the firm's longer-term prospects are positive is necessary to good performance; ambitious, competent job candidates typically apply only to financially sound companies strategically placed for increasing market share.

Clearly, part of management's job—individually and collectively—is to share enough strategic thinking to satisfy employees that the corporate vision is clearly defined. If management does not satisfy this "(emotional) need/right to know," people will be inclined to explore external opportunities, further distracting them from their work.

Fun: People are much more likely to remain committed to an institution and continue to perform well when one very simple condition is met—they are having fun!

An enjoyable, stimulating environment is often at the top of an employee's list of job criteria; she may give up some financial compensation or upward mobility to maintain it.

Take away that fun, and the changes are sudden and dramatic. Why would anyone elect to give ground on compensation or mobility, if the job isn't going to be fun anymore? The answer is simple: the smart ones won't stick around. When was the last time you heard "It just wasn't fun anymore!" as the impetus for leaving a position?

Personal Dignity and Respect: It's possible to be well paid, clear about the firm and its plans, and still feel victimized. If the firm treats a person as if his presence and contributions are unworthy, he is likely to be offended and consider leaving. Yes, immediate practical considerations or the lure of money may induce a person to stay for a time; eventually, the need for respect and appreciation will prevail.

One stereotypical workplace infamous for significant pecuniary benefits but an abusive environment is Wall Street. Wave after wave of young and ambitious university graduates feed into the Wall Street machine, where they spend as many years as they can stand working horribly long hours, subjected to a hostile and, at times, racist and sexist atmosphere. The average tenure in years may be counted on the fingers of just one hand. The money is seductive and keeps them enthralled *until* their personal maturity helps them realize their dignity is worth more than the paycheck beguiling them to stay in an emotionally (and sometimes physically) unhealthy setting.

Sense of Control: Numerous studies show that all humans have an inherent need for a sense of control; some have an extremely limited ability to tolerate ambiguity. Indecision, agitation, frustration, tension and anxiety are common among people who have little or no say in what work they do, or when, where, how, or with whom they must share the work environment.

Individuals who believe they have only responsibility and no authority, or have no autonomy in even small tasks can become very "high maintenance" employees, exhibiting traits in common with people victimized in other settings. Crime victims, for example, are distinguished by their resentful, fearful response to being helpless. Even if not physically or financially harmed, a victim's emotional outrage stems from having their control forcibly taken, leaving them defenseless, at another's mercy.

When events spiral out of control, it's natural to wonder what will happen next, and to try to gain some understanding and sense of certainty. When even a small certainty proves elusive, the sense of helplessness—and the outrage, depression, or shame associated with it—deepens. Eventually deciding the only solution is to get away from the maddening setting where he is subjected to the whims of fate (or, more likely, bad management) is actually a sign of emotional intelligence: a person who allows himself to be abused lacks self-respect and self-confidence. The longer people believe they are mistreated, the greater their frustration and desperation to regain some control. If those efforts are not successful, they are far more likely to exercise their last options—to walk out the door and never look back. If the frustration and shame result from abusive management practices that violate the law, you may find yourself defending lawsuits and paying penalties long after an employee's departure.

Predicting how a given individual will react to the dysfunction around him is difficult. Some people may be willing to give up one or more of these elemental Drivers as a short-term sacrifice; but in the long-term, their fundamental yearning for fair compensation, direction or certainty, fun, dignity and control will overwhelm even the most dedicated employees. Sometimes people do compromise, usually from necessity. Fun and compensation are the most commonly surrendered, not because these are unimportant, but more because people come to believe that expecting anything better in the dysfunctional situation is unreasonable. Each person has his own emotional "pain threshold"; once it is crossed, he'll begin to perform poorly and/or eventually decide to escape.

Too many managers were taught that the act of putting people in suits transforms them from humans to a pod of grey flannel-clad robots. Such managers believe that "behaving professionally" or "being professional" means denying one's humanity and employees should (robotically) take orders and follow them. Emotional distress is often ignored or simply forbidden. Ignoring people's emotional imperatives leads an organization to self-destruction. Similarly, renewal and revitalization begins with finding good people, creating constructive environments and meeting basic needs for dignity, respect, and personal and professional satisfaction.

When people believe their leaders are committed to them and their well being, they will respond by voluntarily agreeing to compromise on one, perhaps more, of these Drivers, *provided that the sacrifice is well understood, and it's clearly finite.* Dignity and respect are *never* negotiable, *never* to be sacrificed.

Clearly, emotionally competent managers recognize the power of emotional imperatives for themselves and others; they model and enforce mature, constructive behavior that contributes to the firm's prosperity. Mature, courteous adults in the workplace foster environments that support high standards of behavior and accomplishment, effectively discouraging disruptive emotional outbursts and behaviors.

The "Top Twelve" Constructive Human Traits

What makes a person an "asset"? The traits we value and strive to manifest, and hope to find in our colleagues, are:

Competence: Technically and emotionally suitable for his current position, and has the ability and desire to learn, mature, and accept more responsibilities; capable, thinks critically; conscientious;

Attentiveness: Able to concentrate one's attention, focus on a speaker, instructions, or tasks fully; is fully present and engaged;

Loyalty: Deeply felt sense of obligation and commitment to colleagues and the firm's success;

Humility: Modest, unpretentious, and courteous; able to laugh at one's own mistakes, accept responsibility for errors; able to see the humor in difficult situations;

Generosity: Unselfish; one who takes pleasure in seeing others succeed; willing to share one's time, talents, and wealth freely to support one's religious or moral principles;

Frugality: Uses resources to their best advantage; avoids waste; believes it is possible to do more with less and still deliver superior products and services;

Respect: Shows regard for the person, beliefs, ideals of others; refrains from intruding upon another's privacy or personal space; behaves decently toward members of the opposite sex.

Patience: Composed, behaves calmly; demonstrates self-control; ability to think clearly under duress; able to suppress annoyance with delays; uncomplaining, controls his temper;

Charity: Kind, gives others the benefit of the doubt; contributes selflessly to others in need or to boost their confidence;

Diligence: Industrious, self-disciplined; attentive to detail and persistent; requires little supervision;

Merit: Earns others' respect and trust by performing well, keeps promises, and accepts praise or rewards only when deserved;

Tolerance: Fair; willing to accept others' methods of working, opinions and ideas on their own merit; accepts race, religious practices and other superficial differences without prejudice.

None among us is perfect; few, if any of us could manifest *all* these qualities *all* the time. The emotionally competent among us *practice* being patient, attentive, and kind. They stretch their native emotional intelligence to learn tolerance in the face of bigotry, demonstrate their loyalty to their mission, their team, and themselves. They *work at* being peacemakers and facilitators, strive to think and act ethically and morally, especially in times of extreme stress or provocation.

Which of these strengths do you demonstrate most commonly? If you learned that if you worked hard and excelled in school, you would do well professionally, you are among the sadly misled majority. Emotional competencies are generally not taught in universities; being subject literate and having work experience are only minimum qualifications: you can expect everyone else with whom you compete for positions and promotions to have the same essential skills.

Look at the list again: only one mentions technical skill. Why? Numerous studies in the field of emotional intelligence have shown that truly effective workers—from entry-level to CEO—are emotionally competent. Amoco, for example, identifies about *73 percent of the abilities identified for superior performance as emotional competencies.* Other studies, using senior management success criteria only, conclude that up to *90 percent of the requisite skills are emotional competencies.*

Turnaround situations create stresses and challenges; creating supportive, "employee-friendly" environments where people can work effectively and efficiently is a business imperative for successful firms. Encourage and nurture the "Top Twelve" in your human assets, unless you intend to find your workplace populated with their ugly counterparts /corollaries, described below.

The "Dirty Dozen" Destructive Human Traits, Plus One

Why are some people liabilities? They may possess traits such as laziness or ineptitude, or because their (learned) behavior has turned destructive in other ways. Anyone who has spent any time in any office (or in any other setting in which humans interact), has witnessed some combination of the following behaviors or characteristics, which will be called the "Dirty Dozen:"

Ineptitude: Lack of technical skills or experiences to perform one's job adequately: for example, a person who routinely forgets or fails to grasp and take into account important factors, leading to repeated failures.

Absent-mindedness: A person who is unable or unwilling to focus on the business because he is constantly preoccupied or distracted by personal issues, or becomes too personally involved in co-workers' concerns.

Disloyalty: An employee's lack of commitment to his firm's success, such as undermining management authority, investing in a competitor's stock, or spreading false rumors that damage an individual's or the company's reputation internally or externally.

Pride or Vanity: Excessive belief in one's own ability to achieve results; one who makes big decisions or takes unnecessary business risks without consulting his leaders.

Envy: Desire for others' traits, status, or abilities; an individual who is more concerned about the size of a colleague's office than he is about doing his own job competently.

Gluttony: Desire to consume more than one's fair share of the firm's resources; expensing very costly meals while traveling on company business, abusing other perks.

Lust: Exhibiting inappropriate attention towards colleagues; a person who somehow believes he's irresistible to members of the opposite sex, and repeatedly makes advances toward those around him.

Anger: Aggression or resentment directed at others (typically co-workers), seeking vengeance; the person whose motto is "Don't get mad, get even!"

Greed: Desire for material wealth or gain; hunger for power, like the person who bulldozes over colleagues in her efforts to secure product sales and qualify for commissions.

Laziness: Avoiding work; the person who takes every opportunity for a break or disappears from the supervisor's sight.

Sense of Entitlement: Unreasonable assumption that one is owed something by the company; the individual who is convinced that he deserves a full bonus regardless of his, or the firm's, performance.

Prejudice: Unfavorable opinion or attitude about a co-worker, formed prematurely; the person who refuses to collaborate with another because he perceives her incapable for some stereotypical reason.

This particular definition of prejudice is used in order to cast the "Dirty Dozen" as generally destructive but not illegal. The thirteenth—*Criminal Behavior*—captures anything that crosses the line from merely destructive to criminal.

Criminal Behavior. More than any of the other undesirable traits, criminal behavior can be fatal for a company. When lust turns to harassment or prejudice becomes racism or bias against a particular group protected under civil law, the line into illegal behavior is crossed, and the damages will be expensive.

Remember: every civil lawsuit contains the words and idea that the accused (and, by extension, his responsible employer) "knew, or should have known" that his behavior is likely to cause harm or injury to others.

An accountant who mistakes a debit for a credit may be inept—should have known better; an accountant who deliberately labels expenditures as credits in order to enhance the company's annual report is guilty of fraud.

Experience shows that inefficiencies resulting from the Dirty Dozen cause billions of dollars in losses annually. The truly disastrous losses stem from the thirteenth trait: those high-profile, criminally motivated debacles with their well-publicized billion-dollar losses for employees and shareholders, and prison sentences for the guilty managers. Enron, WorldCom, and HealthSouth come immediately to mind.

Clearly, no single volume can fully equip you to deal effectively with a criminal, although honing your emotional competencies will alert you to suspicious behavior. This book will focus on the Dirty Dozen.

The Dirty Dozen includes human traits which have shaped our (less than stellar) behavior for millennia; the Seven Deadly Sins are included in the list, their definitions adapted to the workplace.

Both the "Top Twelve" and the "Dirty Dozen" apply to *all* corporate players: your staff, your management, your clients, your suppliers, and yes—even you.

Take a moment to reflect on these Dirty Dozen "sins" and ask yourself which of these you have been guilty of committing. Next, ask yourself why you came to be guilty, either by omission or commission.

You will likely conclude that your behaviors were not due to some inherent evil streak, but were responses to circumstances, anxieties, and pressures. Furthermore, it's also likely that once these environmental pressures changed, your (temporary) inclination toward destructive behaviors abated.

The primary purpose of this book is to highlight how these undesirable characteristics and behaviors may be causing, or contributing to, much of your firm's dysfunction. Dysfunctional behavior is magnified further when a unit is performing poorly; progressive cycles of mistrust, poor performance, disappointment and departure deepen the dysfunction.

Absent the correct infrastructure and managerial commitment, human assets are surely on a fast track to becoming liabilities. When such dysfunction becomes chronic, it's very difficult to reverse, and can be fatal to an organization. As leader, you are responsible for setting the stage to ensure that discord, anxieties, and pressures are relieved to the extent possible.

Chapter 2

Positive Momentum Is a Matter of Urgency

The previous chapter discussed how people's behaviors can be either assets or liabilities to your turnaround efforts. This chapter reviews some of the high-level challenges you will face in the turnaround situation, emphasizing people-related issues. The chapter begins with a discussion of the sustainable momentum you want to generate, proceeds with the commercial orientation you must instill, and ends with the political machinations you must overcome. Part 4 of this book provides more detailed action items you should consider in effecting the turnaround.

First, consider the main challenge. Your task is turning a backward-facing, dysfunctional unit into a cohesive, forward-looking team with the confidence and tools to succeed. Your job is to convert the negative momentum of failures, disappointments, departures, recriminations, stagnation, inefficiencies, and financial losses into trust and team work to gain positive momentum toward success, innovation, and value-creation.

If you don't yet have the confidence to lead others through such complex change, you may need to rethink your decision to take the job.

More generally, if you don't feel comfortable making up your own mind without succumbing to, or without the support of, external influence, you have more growing to do before taking on a senior management role.

Sustainable Momentum

Positive momentum is difficult to define—that subtle impetus that captures our interest, fires our imagination, keeps us moving toward our goal, buoys our spirits and pushes us to excel for the sheer joy of excelling—and even more difficult to generate.

Hope that new leaders and managers will rescue a failing company can overcome some inertia and generate some initial positive momentum; however, only positive *sustainable* momentum will yield powerful, long-term, cumulative results. If you focus only on numbers, such as revenue or net income at year-end, without adequate consideration for how the teams you are striving to create will earn those dollars, any initial momentum will collapse. Achieving a healthy momentum to bridge the gap between the current crisis and the long-term stability and profitability of the company requires balancing both human and financial capital requirements.

***Example:** Consider a manager who has capital to invest and must choose among several business lines. He may have one mature, profitable business line whose growth is slowing; one small business with high growth rates fueled by enthusiastic management in an underserved market, from which he expects healthy future profit margins.*

He could choose to invest in the mature business, increasing revenue or profit most in the near-term.

Or he could focus on the smaller, more dynamic enterprise which has potential to generate more profit overall, but take longer to produce those dollars—the ubiquitous management dilemma.

Many managers mistake tactics for strategy, making short-term- impact decisions that do not contribute to long-term goals, rather than exercising sufficient will and patience to solidify the longer-term value impact. Many public companies today face this demand for short-term gains: intense scrutiny forces them to manage from quarter-to-quarter rather than over a longer horizon.

One of the qualifying questions you must ask when contemplating a leadership position is whether you, as manager, will be given time to act for maximum value creation, or be forced onto a particular timeline or horizon by shareholders or the Board.

A firm can have positive revenue and profit growth, but still be ailing in a strategic sense; a firm with only modest growth in a fast-growing industry is an example. While this particular firm is growing marginally, competitors are, in contrast, growing by leaps and bounds. Over time, the slower-growing firm will be losing market share and will have far less margin for error in decision-making. This strategic disadvantage can be fatal: marketplace resources such as favorable credit terms, highly qualified staff and choice locations go to the firms with demonstrated positive momentum, leaving the ailing firm with not only diminishing market share, but diminishing opportunity. Avoiding negative momentum requires that you clearly identify the actions necessary to jump-start the stalled momentum.

So how do you, as the leader, identify negative momentum, discern its causes, systematically address them, and begin to score some wins?

- You begin by studying the company as you find it.

- Question everything; continue to ask questions until you fully understand what is, and is not, working;

- As you gain insight, you can prioritize the problems and address the most significant/urgent ones first.

- Knowing *what* doesn't work is often a function of knowing *who* isn't working well;

- Draw on maturity, common sense, and both technical and emotional competencies.

Some words of caution before you unleash your listening skills; a number of forces may interfere with your efforts to collect and make sense of facts:

- There are often several versions of the "truth." The concept of "fact" is a moving target. Be mindful, however, that the presence of stark contradictions can help to focus attention where it is most needed. Your job is to make sure you have enough data, verified, to draw valid conclusions.

- People will naturally "spin" their answers. Be mindful that every person will have a unique perspective, and place their statements within the context of their business experience and maturity. This does not imply malicious intent on their part, although in extreme cases, such as the Enron debacle, people can be dishonest and go to great lengths to cover their own errors of omission or commission.

- In some cases there will be no answers—possibly because a particular question has never been asked before, or because the people who know the answers are no longer available.

- Sometimes, people just need to be heard. They may tend to talk about what is on their minds, and may not necessarily answer your questions. No malice implied, simply human nature. You must be certain you are asking the right questions of the right people.

So, how do you get the information you need to make a proper assessment to empower good decision-making? How do you separate those elusive "facts" from wishful thinking and fiction?

You need to be a sponge for information:

- Examine financial statements thoroughly.

- Study any consultant's reports the Board or senior management may have commissioned in their research to determine whether a turnaround effort is necessary.

- Scrutinize minutes of meetings, paying particular attention to strategic recommendations, whether adopted or not.

- Read every internal and external audit report you can find, particularly those from regulatory agencies.

- Review the text of any relevant legal actions pending against the company.

- Seek internal and external assessments of relevant macroeconomic forces, especially credible commentary about your particular industry.

- Talk with as many people, at as many levels of the company, as you can; thoughtful questions demonstrate that you are seriously seeking their input.

- Use your own professional and social networks to save time gathering information, extend your own expertise or knowledge, and get unbiased, competent feedback from people you trust.

- Use your common sense and—most important of all—be a discerning listener. Listening, in this context, is more than just hearing people's words—it's *understanding* them. Their manners of speech, tone of voice, hesitancy or confidence in what they say are as important as the words chosen.

- *Understanding* what people mean isn't necessarily *agreeing* with them. People know when they're being listened to with respect: it signals that you are paying attention and that you will give their contributions—or lack thereof—serious consideration.

The ability to listen empathetically and objectively is, arguably, *the most important skill a leader or manager can possess.* Empathy—that intellectual ability to identify with others' feelings, thoughts, and attitudes—helps you connect on a deeper level. Once an honest connection is established, most will open up to you and provide more, rather than less, information.

Again, empathizing doesn't mean agreeing. Objectivity on your part is critical because once people talk to you, you still need to distill their information and identify the most relevant and actionable facts.

The need for objectivity applies broadly. The Board or existing management will have ideas about what needs to be done; however, just as you must avoid being overly influenced by any one employee, you must avoid undue influence of a single Board member. Each and every person, regardless of their standing within the institution, has opinions, preferences, and a personal agenda. You are one of them, too! Take the time to investigate and draw your own conclusions; make sure you are not interpreting the facts as you see them in the jaundiced light of your own prejudices and biases.

When you start working toward bringing about a turnaround, it's essential for you to remember that one result of prolonged dysfunction is a deterioration of trust and faith in "the system." When people are concerned about their livelihood, they become much more edgy and sensitive, heightening the probability of overt conflicts, departures and lawsuits—including sexual harassment, poisoned environment, and wrongful termination suits. Complaints to regulatory agencies by employees seeing protection from bad management and their lawsuits against the company are the price of uncertainty and dysfunction—yet another reason why quick action is important once you come on board.

Be mindful; use your powers of observation for signs of percolating stress and take action before problems are too serious to be contained.

Some incoming managers believe they should spend time with their direct reports only—typically the most senior officers of the unit—leaving the remaining employees very few opportunities to be heard. This is not a good start.

A troubled firm's manager is obligated to discover the full extent of the issues faced by the firm. When people sense the boss has no inclination to hear them, they will oblige him by staying away; a critical source of decision-making input is lost. Be accessible; encourage people to share their thoughts with you. Over time, you will be able to distinguish those who have constructive insight from those who do not.

One-on-one sessions and small group meetings with staff can be extremely rewarding, but you must be willing to invest the time to observe and consider your personnel at a deep level. Make a concentrated effort to understand each person's attitudes, moods, dispositions, and intentions. That is, discover their motives and agendas.

This ambitious effort can be quite exhausting; it's natural to run out of steam. Don't stop this process prematurely! Strive to devote equal time to the individuals and business groups relevant to your fact-gathering. Each one deserves an opportunity to inform you, and you can't afford to miss important feedback. Avoid being a manager who realizes, a year into her mandate, she has yet to speak for the first time to a large proportion of her staff.

Learning the causes of individual staff members' anxieties and comparing each individual's concerns to those of the group as a whole will help you discern whether the dysfunction arises from one or two issues, or whether it is systemic.

The very act of speaking their minds and sharing their concerns can be cathartic. Let people go through this process. You may think you have better things to do than spend thirty minutes with a junior person talking about his anxieties, but in many cases, you would be wrong, for at least two reasons:

- People are the heartbeat of an organization: an army is usually run by its sergeants and corporals; middle managers are your corporate body's sergeants and corporals. Ignore them and focus only on colonels and generals, and you will waste precious time and energy.

- It's critical in the turnaround situation that the "water-cooler talk" turn in your favor as soon as possible. There is a huge difference between that first acquaintance describing you as a heartless snob versus someone who is approachable and reasonable. Take advantage of this opportunity to build your stock among your colleagues.

When you speak with people, draw them out. Push them to share with you. This may take some effort—some people will be unable to share simply because of their nature or cultural influences; others may be suspicious, or reluctant to share their deepest concerns and opinions for fear of being wrong(ed).

Historically, some authors have argued that accessibility is not a skill every manager must bring to the table. Approachability is far more critical in a troubled firm than in a financially stable company. The troubled firm's employees are far more in need of reassurance that the new person will help lead them toward salvation. They have a much greater need to interact with the new boss, sense his solidity and dependability. Signals of non-accessibility can very quickly be interpreted as "here's another suit-wearing ass who doesn't really care about us or the business," damaging morale further, while an opportunity to send a positive message has been lost.

More critically, it's impossible to retrieve that first chance at conversation and reassurance. Specifically, keep your door open; tell people you want them to drop by, and be genuinely pleased to see them when they do. Make it your priority to accommodate them if at all possible; apologize sincerely and name a concrete alternative meeting times if the timing is not good. Set aside sufficient time to be fully engaged in conversations; focus your full attention on each speaker, relax, and consider whether any of your physical actions or verbal comments may be (mis)interpreted as impatient, biased or prejudiced.

Control your own communications; decide for yourself who to talk with, and when. If you get the impression that your immediate circle is purposefully restricting your access to "their people," alarm bells should be going off in your head.

Accessibility is an accurate measure of an organization's transparency; those who restrict it are not serving the organization's overall good, but obfuscating their own agendas to the detriment of the firm.

Commercial Orientation

People feel better about themselves and perform at a high level when they believe in their company's professionalism. Successful firms consistently exhibit an important trait–commercial orientation: every person in the firm, regardless of role, understands that he is part of a business and is sufficiently professional to do his part, especially when facing clients or prospects. Obviously, sales people need to know how to sell, marketers need to know how to put together a marketing campaign: commercial orientation means that a receptionist behaves professionally when a prospect is accidentally transferred on a phone line; a janitor knows it's important to politely redirect a client who is wandering in the hallways, hopelessly lost.

In contrast, when a commercial orientation is missing, people tend to under-perform. The receptionist hangs up on people, the janitor ignores lost visitors, product managers don't strive for excellence, and consultants no longer take pride in providing the best, most creative, advice to clients.

Everyone is, at all times, an ambassador of the firm to the outside world. Everyone sells, everyone markets, everyone advertises, everyone identifies production flaws, everyone pays attention to client needs; firms that achieve this level of professionalism and focus do much better than those that do not.

Many firms, distressed firms among them, have intriguing products but lack market orientation: even good products won't sell if the firm can't connect properly with its client base. This is relevant in any industry, but is especially prevalent in fields such as high-tech and biotech.

Brilliant ideas, inventions, and products, when owned and managed by engineers unable to make the leap from an academic research environment to a commercially-oriented enterprise, are wasted, eating up huge amounts of investor capital, earning very little revenue in the process.

Lack of commercial orientation represents just one deficiency among many for ailing firms; the good news for a firm lacking commercial orientation is that it can be pursued in parallel to solving other challenges.

Thus, while many dysfunctions are intertwined and difficult to identify and resolve, commercial orientation, which is very much a mindset, can be taught and nurtured independent of other required solutions. In fact, a commercial mindset will help to solve other problems.

The key is for you to identify the lack of awareness, then to systematically ensure that those staff members who do have the correct mindset educate and train their colleagues. If such people are not present in the firm, add "commercial orientation" to the required emotional competencies for candidates to fill open positions.

Alternatively, and if practical, you may serve as the educator for one group of employees, who can, in turn, disseminate that knowledge to others.

Recognizing and Deflecting Political Machinations

The political lobbying will begin your first hour on the job. Remember: you are coming into a dysfunctional situation; everyone will have opinions, whether or not they are willing to state them directly. You must be a good, intuitive judge of character and behavior.

Character shows most clearly in times of stress; push your senior managers into stressful situations and see how they react. Do they exhibit leadership? Do they blame others? Do people naturally rally around them? Do junior people trust them?

Example: *The most extreme tests of character may be those employed by spy agencies. By necessity, these organizations must ensure that they have a true understanding of a candidate's strengths and weaknesses. The challenge is that most people, consciously or subconsciously, hide certain personality traits, often because of fears that some traits may not be welcomed or appreciated by a particular audience.*

The tests must, therefore, reveal true character. Typical tests involve a small number of candidates, and a relatively large number of professional observers, often a selection of field officers and psychologists. For example, there may be four candidates and a dozen observers. Over the course of several days, the candidates may be divided into competing groups, or asked to respond to various questions. There is no physical hardship involved. The challenges are all intellectual. By design, there is much ambiguity involved in the outlined challenges, and there are no absolutely correct solutions or answers. While the candidates are progressively subjected to more and more stress—some of it self-imposed due to their competitive natures—the observers are looking for what causes lowered defenses and how individuals exhibit their lack of self-mastery.

Eventually, as the stress builds, true character traits are revealed. People begin to snap at each other, there are spontaneous outbursts and finger-pointing.

Needless to say, these extreme "cloak and dagger" techniques are not appropriate for a corporate setting. There is, however, some merit in arranging an offsite for a selection of key personnel, and subjecting them to challenges that tease out character and personality traits which may not be obvious in the usual office setting.

Avoid the temptation to confide in *anyone* early on; your natural inclination might lead you to someone who *appears* to be a solid member of the executive team. The danger is that a personable executive has the wits and political will to charm and deceive, and is overlooked when seeking the cause of the firm's problems. Choosing the wrong person as your confidant early on can be deadly, as your entire perception of the company and its problems may be skewed, costing you your only chance at success.

Push back on your boss or the Board early on to signal your independence and test your limits. If you disagree with a recommendation, avoid statements such as "I think you're wrong!" Acknowledge the merit in others' suggestions, and explain why you believe a different approach may be in order, or perhaps why a different sequence of actions may be more effective. As you make your counter arguments, observe the reactions of your audience. Are your arguments well-received? If not, perhaps judicious retreat is in order. If your suggestions appear to be well-received, you may elect, respectfully, to seek even more concessions for your preferred solutions. At some point, it's likely the audience will provide very obvious or more subtle cues making it clear that your suggestions are well outside their comfort zone. Hammering on desktops, yelling, and door-slamming would be some of the more obvious signals of dissatisfaction, while the more subtle cues may include frowning, fidgeting, reluctance to make eye contact, or complete silence. These are your cues to stop pushing, and consolidate any gains achieved.

Your power and bargaining position will fade over time if there aren't clear signs of success. Use your good standing early on to renegotiate or revise expectations, particularly if your initial research shows the dysfunction has been underestimated or its causes incorrectly identified.

As a senior executive you will have to deal with technical and non-technical people, in both functional and support departments. You may find yourself out of your depth in discussing details of finance and accounting, administration, sales, marketing, development, research, legal, information technology (IT), and so on. The more you know in each of these fields, the more self-sufficient you will be, the fewer people you will need to rely upon, and the faster you can orient yourself and make good decisions.

A well-rounded executive brings a powerful combination of skills, and continues to hone them for her entire career. It's easy to hate accounting and avoid it like the plague, but you will wish you hadn't skipped that accounting class the first time you have to dive into the smallest details of a poorly performing business. You need not be a legal or IT expert, but having enough knowledge to spot inconsistencies can be very helpful. People will shape "facts" to suit their own agendas. The more knowledge and skill you have, the better your ability to separate fact from fiction. Over time, as long as you remain vigilant, your "radar" will be more refined.

As you conduct your reviews, include experts whose competence and ethics you can rely on; their expertise is most useful if there is nothing at stake for them in a given conversation. The closer your probing goes to their own activities, the more likely they will become subjective. Keep this in mind as you involve them, and sprinkle salt liberally over their feedback.

Are people being too conservative in their estimates and actions? This may occur in isolated fashion (a particular project), or on a larger scale (consistent behavior by individuals or groups). The risks in certain cases may well justify conservatism. In some cases, however, the conservatism reflects a "cover your ass" (CYA) approach, and may be deliberate obfuscation. You must get to the bottom (no pun intended) of such behavior, as persistent conservatism can be a sign of ineptitude and/or lack of knowledge or understanding. Do recognize that the CYA behavior may be a response to inconsistent or poor leadership in the past. Thus, while you notice such behavior, don't immediately condemn people if, or when, you observe it.

The points made at the beginning of this section bear repeating:

- People will try to impress you when you first arrive: they will jockey for position and attempt to influence your decision-making in favor of their agendas.

- The most eloquent lobbyists may not necessarily be the bearers of the most accurate or reliable information: they may *sound* more credible than others due to their superior communication skills.

- The politically inclined will make their case: less politically-motivated individuals probably wouldn't see the benefit of being aggressive.

- Keep in mind that the firm is likely ailing precisely because the wrong people are exerting influence.

- Fortunately, efforts to exert influence over you will typically settle down (somewhat) once you make it clear that you are politically astute and refuse to be manipulated.

Example: *Here's an example of a new CEO of a small firm of about one hundred people. The CEO, who came from outside the firm, made decisions early on to trust a vocal subset of his inner circle. He removed others on the advice of the vocal subset. The problem was that he listened to the wrong crowd, falling prey to their eloquent but self-serving arguments. They painstakingly rehearsed their messages, and the resulting consistency of their statements made them appear more credible.*

Within six months of embracing their recommendations, things were falling apart. An early symptom was a wave of departures of junior personnel; though young and less-experienced, they saw the writing on the wall. When the people they admired were removed, in favor of people they didn't respect, the exodus was on. These departures, at a critical time, led to an inability to deliver certain high-profile projects and damaged the firm's reputation. Furthermore, the desperate need to find replacements meant that management had to focus on recruiting precisely at a time when their time should have been spent elsewhere—for example, on building the future revenue pipeline. Meanwhile, as the CEO was struggling to put out brushfires, the inner circle were making exit plans. Eventually, the new CEO was left with a burned-out shell.

There is a very simple moral to this story: *Don't listen to the wrong people!* Exercise good judgment and heed your intuition to discern who is credible, and who is not.

You were brought in to fix something: you have, by definition, walked into a mess. One of the predictable tendencies for your middle managers and executives will be to blame the current state of affairs on others. Ironically, those with more integrity will be reluctant to point fingers, while the less-scrupulous will be the first to undermine their colleagues. Do not condemn people who are concerned about their own careers and families; it is a natural instinct: anyone whose motives are *not* concerned with family and career is suspect. You must reprimand dishonesty; however, the personal perspective is the only one available to us; it's your job to find any fallacies clouding their perspective, examine them objectively, draw valid conclusions, and act fairly.

Your hire represents a change in the balance of power; individuals will feel empowered or disenfranchised, depending upon where they were in the old power structure. Some less-capable people will avoid or delay the day of reckoning by keeping a low profile and riding things out. This is usually a tactic used by veterans who know how "the game" is played. They may wait for you to run into trouble, and come out of their lairs when you are weakened. Take action early on to identify and convert or remove such people.

Example: *Following a sweeping, high-level managerial review, a unit based in an isolated, geographically-distant office was determined to have outdated skills, holding it back from making contributions to other parts of the firm.*

An instruction to the unit's local manager to provide up-to-date training met with resistance. At management's subsequent urging, the immediate manager pretended to go along with the reforms, providing reports carefully crafted to give the impression of collaboration.

Behind the scenes, however, the local manager allowed the unit to continue its insular habits. Simultaneously, the local manager ingratiated himself with senior managers in the remote location, knowing they harbored general resentment toward corporate senior management.

This unholy alliance allowed the unit in question to resist change for over a year, at which point other priorities distracted corporate senior management from its initial goal of reform. The upstart group, recognizing the (unintended) reprieve, and knowing that management was sufficiently distracted elsewhere, returned to overtly pursuing its outdated agenda.

Expect factions: try to identify them early. Groups become factions when dissensions arise over compensation mechanisms, cultural inclinations, regional affiliations or other elements of corporate life. Firms stitched together from several corporate acquisitions will tend to have cliques with a natural predisposition to distrust other cliques; some of these groups may well have been arch competitors in the past. As they jockey for position and resources in the new firm, they will naturally gravitate to their old friendships, dividing the firm into "us-versus-them" factions.

Your challenge is to lead all people to cooperate and form a new, unified company identity. The first step in dealing with factions is identification.

- Factions typically consist of a fiefdom of people at several levels of seniority, often led by one or several powerful figures within the organization.

- The wielders of power may be in the foreground, or behind the scenes; but, their common trait is an ability to embed a particular mindset in their crowd, usually one which sees all others within the firm as untrustworthy.

- Some factions are obvious by their frequent physical gatherings and alliances during open debates, others when they congregate in whispered conversation which abruptly (and guiltily) stops when outsiders approach.

- Factions may be formed by an executive who hires a number of former colleagues, stacking his deck with loyal followers.

- Members of a faction may be identified by extreme collegiality outside the workplace. You'd be wise to be aware of any tight-knit and insular group of people who play golf together, or bond in any other activity to which other colleagues are clearly unwelcome.

Once you have identified the factions, wean them away from viewing colleagues within the firm as "them"; establish clearly that the only "them" of concern are external competitors.

Once you have identified the faction leaders, a frank discussion may be all that is necessary for an employee to be loyal and productive. Involve him constructively with appropriate responsibilities and challenges that make him *want* to be a member of your team. Once he buys into your vision and approach, his followers will do the same.

If the faction leaders are unable to convince their followers to "get with the new program," your next step is to divide and conquer. Separate the faction into smaller groups, severing their old comfortable ties; replace those ties with functional responsibilities where they can build more constructive relationships and new loyalties to the company Mission.

The harsh truth is that not everyone will see the value in your vision or a united purpose; those who refuse to follow management directions can be allowed to resign; failure to tender resignation should result in termination of their employment.

Strive to identify any personal connections between your employees and senior members of the corporation who are outside your business unit or division. Such connections may stem from friendships, family relationships, fraternal organizations or other interests. When these "insiders" among your staff embrace your vision, they can help you persuade skeptics among senior "outsiders."

On the other hand, the "insiders" can be a thorn in your side—or a dagger in your back. "Insiders" may be a fifth column planted by senior management or the Board to monitor your activities.

Example: I ran into a manager of a large and very profitable corporation. He had one Achilles heel; a unit he had formed years before, on which he had bet a lot of political capital, had been losing money for years. Given his natural inclination for Machiavellian intrigue, and the added pressure of his pet project losing a lot of money, he made a habit of planting his personal confidantes (read "spies") in the smaller unit. Each new manager of the unit would take a few months to realize that information was being leaked directly to the senior manager, and each eventually decided he didn't want to live with this "assassin." The unit went through four managers in twelve months.

You will make political enemies with your first decision. Beware those (enemies) who stir dissension; their early backstabbing will be weak compared to your relative strength, but any lack of progress on your plans (even *apparent* lack of progress) will allow their agitations to gradually take hold.

Eventually, the political dissenters could cause you to fail, especially if they are well-connected in the corporation. Identify the agitators early; neutralize their influence or remove them as soon as practicable, making it clear to dissenters and their allies, regardless of their corporate power, that undermining the authority of the executive leadership team cannot be tolerated. It's far easier to justify their removal early on, when no one can accuse you of politicking. Later, especially if your plans suffer some setbacks, the agitators can make it appear that you are trying to silence them (to avoid having legitimate concerns aired), making it much more difficult for you to prevail.

PART TWO
ASSESS the FIRM'S CURRENT STATE

CHAPTER 3

Evaluate Individual and Collective Performances

Before embarking on this section, one reminder is in order. The chapters in this Part address evaluation and assessment of processes, plans, and staff performance. Action items for remedying and observed deficiencies may be found in Part 4.

In a turnaround situation, gaining an understanding of people—their strengths and weaknesses, concerns and aspirations—must be among your highest priorities.

Every staff member's performance must be reviewed; this doesn't mean you have to meet each person personally, unless the firm is small enough. Personally conduct as many performance interviews as possible, especially all managers; one critical measure of a manager's performance is his first-person knowledge of the individuals and teams who report directly to him, particularly those you can't meet personally.

One way to gauge how people perform under stress is in a challenging client meeting. Fortunately (or unfortunately), such meetings are too common at an ailing firm; there are usually unhappy clients who want to vent their frustration, renegotiate contracts, or at least register their displeasure face-to-face with a decision-maker.

Look for people who are inclined to engage challenging clients constructively, take responsibility for resolving issues, and satisfy others that their concerns are taken seriously. Everyone likes easy meetings. The most commendable employees are those willing to attend and actively participate in the hard meetings (with irate clients or partners), seeking the best outcome for the firm.

As you evaluate your direct reports' performance, concentrate on four elements:

- Their individual skills,

- Their managerial and leadership skills,

- Their integrity, and,

- Whether they are value-creators or value-destroyers.

Evaluating Individual Skills

Every employee must possess the core capabilities necessary to meet the minimum requirements of his job description. Managers, especially in distressed firms, must possess sufficient technical skills to teach new staff, help existing staff develop their skills, and fill-in on short notice for departed or absent staff quickly and seamlessly. Determine the extent of your direct reports' skills by considering:

Core Skills: The *minimum academic* requirements for *any* job are the ability to read, write, and do math commensurate with the position, competently.

The *minimum* non-academic capabilities for *any* job are oral and written communication skills, interpersonal skills, and initiative.

Integrity, dependability, and practical expertise set the desirable candidates apart from those who meet only minimum standards for core skills.

Job-related Skills: What specific job-related skills does the employee have, or not have? Consider skills required by his job description. Strong presentation and communication skills are a necessity for salespeople; traveling and working on the road, outside the structured office environment, requires self-discipline.

A quantitative researcher must master complex technical mathematical and analytical processes; he must pay attention to detail.

A client service person has to understand how to resolve technical problems, have a very sunny disposition, tact, a sense of humor, and outstanding communications skills.

Each role requires technical skills and educational qualifications, but the more important skills—learned skills that are not necessarily academic—are emotional skills, which require innate emotional intelligence, mindfulness, and the ability to observe and learn.

Unfortunately, emotional skills are taught in very few academic settings beyond kindergarten; given this lack of emphasis, even exposure, to notions such as empathy and sharing/cooperation, sufficient maturity to be an effective worker are more difficult and time-consuming to develop in the workplace.

Poise: What can he handle or not handle? This question is essentially about instinct, poise, and judgment. Does he know how to phrase an answer to a client? Does he get flustered easily during meetings, in front of clients? Is he tactful? Does he know when to refer issues to more senior people? Does he have the confidence to speak up? Has the person overcome adversity in the past? Is he resilient? Has he shown an ability to recover gracefully from a career setback?

Manners: Does he possess appropriate social graces or manners? Does he seem to care about how his behavior is viewed by others? Does he appear to be sensitive to the fact that different cultures may have different expectations regarding manners and what may be viewed as respectful and respectable behavior by a host?

Aptitude: What aptitudes does he have; is he able and/or inclined to learn other core or specific skills? Is he committed to continual personal and professional growth, or does he seem closed to the idea? Willingness to improve is critical: it's not a crime for a person to be missing certain skills; most technical skills can be taught to anyone who possesses the basic intellect to understand. Is he willing to fill-in for others, accept a lateral reassignment or relocate? The more willing to learn and adapt, the more valuable he is to an evolving organization.

Collaboration Skills: Is the person unselfish, willing to forgo his own preferences for the good of the team? Has he grumbled and pouted, or been gracious? Is he able to understand problems, see patterns, develop ideas? Is he sufficiently open-minded to truly explore novel solutions?

Development: What tasks can be assigned to him to help develop his current skills and learn new ones? Who should teach him?

Evaluating Managerial and Leadership Performance

Managerial and leadership skills are necessary in every firm to ensure that solid decisions are made and staff is deployed most productively. Setting priorities is especially critical for a troubled firm: resource scarcity limits the projects that can be undertaken; selecting the correct ones has existential ramifications because every ounce of productivity matters. A manager must know her staff well, place them for maximum productivity, and inspire them when their morale is low.

In order to evaluate how adept your direct reports are, ask yourself these following questions about each of them:

Ability to Evaluate Others' Performance: How well does she know her direct reports, their capabilities and deficiencies? Has she formulated a development plan for them? How good is the plan? These abilities are critical for any firm desperately trying to build up its leadership capabilities.

Mentoring: Is the person an unselfish mentor? Does she consistently work to develop others? Do they believe she is directing them properly and helping them to obtain the skills and experiences they need to prosper?

Leading: Is she a capable leader? Does she understand the corporate vision, inspire others, gain their trust and confidence? Do her direct reports respect her?

Following: Does she know when to follow? Effective leaders have a sense of when to step back and urge others to lead, learn, gain experience, and confidence; when to step forward and assume the mantle of leadership, without imposing themselves or their status. *Nurture people with these capabilities: they are very rare.*

Managing: Is the person a competent manager? Are her instructions clear, her project plans comprehensive and orderly? Does she understand how to allocate resources, manage a budget to best advantage?

Development Needs: What tasks can be assigned to the manager to help develop her leadership, managerial, or mentoring skills? Who should teach her; should she attend outside educational workshops or job-share with another manager?

With these considerations in mind, you must decide whether each employee is in the correct position given her skills and/or aspirations and the company's broader needs.

Integrity

Integrity is the glue that holds human relationships together. In a corporate environment, belief in one another's integrity encourages people to work toward common goals, in mutually supportive fashion.

Confidence in others' integrity supports positive momentum: projects proceed more smoothly; if co-workers didn't have this mutual trust, productivity would grind to a halt. People's respect for each other and inclination to work together plummet when integrity is missing; everyone would demand written contracts for everything.

Integrity implies a degree of selflessness, trust that a colleague will not take undue credit for one's work, unfairly undermine another's promotion prospects or fail to feed the coffee kitty.

Suffering, anxiety and disappointment rooted in poor management may tempt some to compromise their integrity in an effort to get ahead, or to avoid repercussions for failure. Integrity is a moral imperative, just as respect and dignity are psychological imperatives. People with integrity will not fail their co-workers; they will deal honestly and fairly with each other, as well as with clients and partners; they can be relied upon to do the right thing in the most tempting situations.

When contemplating a person's integrity, ask yourself the following questions:

- Have you ever suspected a person has not told the truth?

- Has this feeling come up on more than one occasion?

- Does he engage in finger pointing; does he readily blame others for mistakes and failures? Does he accept responsibility for negative outcomes or only for positive outcomes?

- Does he take credit for success that may not be his own?

- Do suspicious events occur in close proximity to this person?

- Do you sometimes feel you're not being told all pertinent information?

- Do you sometimes feel his opinions swing around radically, without a clear explanation as to why?

- Do you have a haunting sense that you can't fully believe him? This does not refer to disagreement, but rather to your feeling that *he* doesn't believe what he's saying, either.

- Does he treat those around him fairly and consistently? Does he treat his superiors with exaggerated deference or flattery, while treating his juniors rudely or disrespectfully?

- Does he cheat on a partner or spouse?

- Does he tell lies?

- Does he mislead clients?

- Does the person mistreat colleagues?

Review the list and ask the same questions about yourself.

Integrity is something you either have, or don't have. There should be no distinction between small and large infractions. It's your duty as leader to identify integrity-deficient people and to remove them as soon as possible. Their presence poisons everyone else's environment, and you can ill-afford this in a turnaround situation.

Value-Creators and Value-Destroyers

Value-creators are those who contribute positively to the firm's growth and well-being. Value-destroyers are those who undermine others' efforts, waste resources, and behave dishonestly. Value-creators represent a good return on investment for the firm; value-destroyers, a loss on investment.

Employees who do their job well, pull their weight, innovate, collaborate and fit in socially with their peers are emotionally competent and productive. Those who stifle others' creativity and enthusiasm, complain endlessly, cause delays, produce flawed outputs and generally undermine the firm's efforts (consciously or subconsciously) must reform or be removed.

In some cases, it's easy to identify value-destroyers, but the most insidious ones are not easy to pin down. Some trouble-making types you are will likely encounter are:

Prima Donna: The *Prima Donna* destroys value by demanding attention and resources.

Eternal Pessimist and Morale Depressor: The eternal pessimist always sees the cup half-empty; his consistently dark attitude depresses the morale of others around him, affecting their productivity.

Liar or Cheater: The liar or cheater chronically distorts the truth, creating confusion and frustration among colleagues, and/or engages in illegal behavior which may include theft or fraud.

Distinguishing the creators from the destroyers is important in any firm, but especially in an ailing one. A turnaround firm can't afford inefficiency. It can't afford to carry people who not only do not contribute, but actually cause damage by taking up resources, producing inferior-quality products and services and having conflicts with colleagues. Carrying the deadweight of value-destroyers only exacerbates morale problems; allowing them to continue unchecked hastens the decline of a failing firm.

Some value-destroyers act without malice, exhibiting Dirty Dozen traits such as ineptitude, absent-mindedness, or gluttony. The *Prima Donna* is a glutton, by definition. Others, such as liars and cheats, act maliciously, often expertly hiding the damage they cause

In order to distinguish a creator from destroyer, ask yourself the following questions:

- Do his projects end successfully or unsuccessfully?

- Does he pull his weight or let others do most, or all, of the work?

- Do others resist working with him?

- Do others resent working with him?

- Do his direct reports appear to be poorly-trained and resist having him as a mentor?

- Do his direct reports fail to successfully move on to higher responsibilities?

- Can any of his successes be attributed to other people?

- When volunteers are needed for a project, does he hide?

Be cautious when you suspect a value-destroyer is acting illegally. Consult with senior human resource staff; they will discuss the matter with legal advisors to ensure your efforts, or intended efforts, are within the law and are acceptable practice. The human resources staff is responsible for any confidential investigation of employee behavior, working with internal auditors, and taking any steps necessary to document the illegal behavior.

Avoid the inclination to get too personally involved; confidential investigations are tangential to your job and distracting; human resource professionals are responsible for protecting you and other innocent employees from physically or verbally abusive co-workers.

Evaluating performance—whether an employee is your direct report or at a lower level—you should consider two questions:

- Is he transparent in his dealings? Transparency is a sign of confidence and having nothing to hide.

- Are his patterns of behavior consistent? A pattern of outstanding performance is more suspicious than a pattern of poor behavior: people don't fake failure, but they do fake success.

Example: I recall the CEO of a Wall Street investment bank describing internal procedures he implemented within his firm following the Barings Bank collapse (which was due to rogue trading): if a trader significantly outperformed his peers over the course of a year, he would congratulate him and give him a great bonus. If he outperformed significantly again the next year, the CEO would, in his own words, "audit his ass." The logic? When an achievement appears consistently superhuman, it usually is!

One of your most immediate challenges as the new leader is to quickly identify senior people who represent an obstacle to progress. Your challenge will be compounded by the fact that these very people may *initially* appear to be very positive, loyal contributors. They may display outstanding "smooth talking" skills and may be able to make it appear that the unit's travails are the fault of others.

How do you separate fact from fiction or half-truths?

- First, develop basic intuition to identify sycophantic and other insincere behaviors.

- Do not allow yourself to be flattered or finessed into a compromising position; keep your distance and don't be won over emotionally.

- Early on, it may be very difficult to identify senior managers who are performing poorly, especially as they may do their utmost to restrict your access to incriminating evidence.

Given all the other distractions you will face, it may be difficult to realize what is happening.

So what can you do?

Look for patterns. Good indications that a manager is destroying, rather than creating value, come through in:

Poor Results: Consistently poor results are the most obvious sign of a manager's failure. It usually doesn't take a rocket scientist to conclude that a unit is losing a lot of money and/or consistently failing to achieve its objectives. Even when the manager in question attempts to hide these facts, a thorough performance evaluation should lead you to the truth.

Significant Staff Turnover: The most telling indication of management failure is significant staff turnover. One departure means little, because it can be caused by any one of a dozen or more factors.

A pattern of departures from one person's team is not conclusively damning evidence against the manager in question, but it does call for further investigation, including careful debriefing of departed employees.

HR staff should be able to identify disturbing patterns; exit interviews where the right questions are asked are one part of the process of investigating the reasons for the turnover.

Do not allow the "suspected" manager to perform exit interviews alone. You and/or the HR staff should also speak with those who were closest to each departing employee and most likely to know the real reasons behind decisions to leave.

To get a better sense of the history preceding your arrival, work with HR personnel to obtain a comprehensive list of all employee departures or reassignments over the previous two or three years (or more if available) and look for patterns. Did most of them report to a particular supervisor or manager? Did many people leave suddenly? Did this coincide with the appointment of a particular candidate to a more senior role? These observations alone are not sufficient evidence to implicate the manager, but sufficient reason to observe more closely and keep notes. Weigh their comments carefully; strive to validate some or all of the information they provide—seeking inconsistencies.

Lack of Transparency: Over time, you may realize that you have no idea what a particular manager's team does. In the normal course of events, you'd have some contact with junior employees and some sense of their projects, working conditions and performance.

A complete lack of transparency is unnatural and may reflect the manager's efforts to purposely keep from you any knowledge of his staff and their state of mind. When communications are conspicuously absent, or when you are already questioning the manager's methods or results, go out of your way to spend some time with his junior people.

Always consult HR staff with employee performance–related matters; if there are complaints or negative comments coming from a group, human resources staff will very likely know it before you do. Human resources can find out what the manager's people are actually doing (are they doing what the manager claims they are doing?), gauge their feelings toward their manager, and report to you confidentially.

Your act of reaching out to employees may cause a manager to react defensively, or question your motives; be certain you are not acting out of inappropriate suspicion or prejudice. Be honest, and draw your conclusions carefully.

As you proceed with performance reviews, look for junior people who exhibit significant management and leadership potential; advance them into more responsible positions as soon as is prudent. Their natural ability to create value will be magnified further through their direct reports. Make it known to every other manager, supervisor, or lead person responsible for performance evaluations, as well as human resources staff, that identifying talented junior people is a priority.

Your leadership by example should influence others; candid, professional performance evaluations signal employees that their loyalty and hard work are valued and recognized. Participating with and observing your people evaluating others' performances will also help you to learn about them as leaders and managers.

Impromptu approaches so common in poorly-performing firms invariably mean that employees don't receive a truly representative review of their performance. There's only one description for this—bad people management.

Inexperienced management can be as disastrous as incompetent management. Even when managers are not rushed through the process, inexperience may lead them to deliver less-than-honest messages, systematically biased to the positive end of the spectrum.

Some reasons for this behavior are:

- Desire to avoid confrontation. Managers must have a spine, and they can't shy away from managerial responsibilities. Delivering an honest review need not be a confrontational event. When a manager is consistently honest with an employee and holds ongoing performance discussions (not just one session at year-end), there should be no surprise, no shock, and no confrontation.

- Lack of certainty about what the employee has done, often due to lack of managerial attention. This is inexcusable. A manager must pay continual attention to her people and their development. She can't make up for a year of neglect in one day or one week.

- A concern the employee, who fills a critical role, may leave if the feedback is too harsh. A manager can't be held hostage to what she thinks any single employee may, or may not, do. It's tempting to believe that certain people are indispensable, but history clearly shows everyone is dispensable (and this includes you). If there's reason to believe that a person in a critical role may depart, contingency plans should be set up to lower the firm's dependence on him.

- Failure to maintain personal distance from the employee. Managers must remain emotionally unattached. It's easier to avoid getting too close than to have to reverse that intimacy at a later date.

Providing inflated positive feedback may seem easier in the short-term, but in the longer-term, it hurts the staff and the firm. The dishonest feedback deprives employees of an opportunity to identify deficiencies and work on improving their skills. This, in turn, means they won't improve in areas most critical to the firm: therefore, the firm won't be progressing. Furthermore, the staff will find themselves in an even worse state when they do finally encounter a manager (in the same firm or elsewhere) who provides honest assessments.

There is often an assumption that employees won't notice that little effort has been made in the review process, or that the feedback provided to them is insincere. In fact, people quite easily sense when their review is insincere or viewed as low priority. This leads them to question the commitment being made by the firm to their development, and ultimately to erosion of trust and loyalty. Conversely, people can tell when a sincere effort has been made to provide meaningful feedback. Even in those cases where the feedback includes some (constructive) criticism, the honesty is appreciated and respected.

Stretching People

As the leader, it's up to you to get the most out of people.

Some schools of thought interpret pushing people to the limit as old-fashioned, uncaring, and exploitative. "Stretching people" does not imply taking unfair advantage: it means challenging and simultaneously teaching them about their own capacity for thinking, problem solving, and executing. Throw in fair compensation and you are contributing socially—not exploiting anyone.

In many ways, the ultimate stretching experiences are military basic training courses. These incredibly intense experiences force all participants to dig very deep within themselves and deal constructively with what they find. As a starting point, each person has to contend with stripping away from their value system all consideration of the individual, and submit completely to the greater good—essentially subjugating personal impulses to a new hierarchy of priorities: "God, Country, Unit" or some equivalent sentiment.

The military is able to utilize techniques unacceptable in the commercial sector. Most people in a business setting would not respond well to being told they can't go home for months on end, have to give up washing for weeks at a time, must give up food occasionally, and submit to seemingly humiliating experiences at the hands of heartless Non-Commissioned Officers.

Pushing people in a commercial setting to set their goals and targets higher, to be more alert, to be more proactive, to be more team-oriented is reasonable. The most effective "push" is to create a culture that values excellence and collaboration and rewards those who embrace these values.

Example: *Early in my managerial career, I came into a unit that was struggling significantly. The members of the team were defeated, demoralized, and depressed. After taking in this scene for several weeks I addressed the unit in a town* *hall setting. I talked to them about excellence. I made it clear that the only way, in my opinion, to achieve our goals was to go for the win, and not to settle for anything other than wrenching first place from the most feared competitor.*

This was a reflection of a very closely-held belief on my part: if you are in last place, the only way to improve meaningfully is to focus on, and aim for, first place. If you do this intensely, two things may happen: one, you may win, a wonderful outcome for all concerned; two, you may not come in first, but your intense and focused pursuit of excellence will probably vault you into the elite circle of players. Looking back at where you came from, this is also a solid and respectable achievement.

As I wound up my discussion, a very senior person put up his hand and publicly said that, given how badly things had gone in the past, he'd be happy if the unit could make it into the middle of the pack.

Here's another closely held belief of mine: if you shoot for mediocrity, at best you will be mediocre, but more likely you'll continue to settle for the same deflationary arguments you've accepted in the past, and end up somewhere below mediocre. I subscribe to the school of thought that says: "Go hard or go home!"

Soon thereafter, the senior person quoted above was gone. By the end of the next full year, the unit had doubled its revenue and reduced expenses by over a third; there were a lot of eager new faces in the office and momentum and morale were on the rise. We were becoming a force to be reckoned with.

Once you've successfully instilled confidence in the staff, it's much easier to challenge them to reach higher and higher. Ideally, it will become a matter of pride for people to strive for excellence. A key, of course, is to continue to set challenges, but ensure they're achievable. It doesn't do anyone good to set impossible goals and then watch failures pile up.

CHAPTER 4
Evaluate Your Company's Performance

Before you can make changes, you have to understand the company's current state; employee performance evaluations will yield a great deal of useful information, particularly if those evaluations are planned and carried out in the context of the existing culture, internal systems and processes, partners, clients, plans and strategy, revenues and external factors (market share, economic conditions, etc.). These elements are assessed in this chapter.

Identify Predominant Culture(s) within the Firm

A firm's culture is a critical determinant of its success or failure. In your case, the firm is in trouble; at least some elements of the corporate culture are not helping the cause, and are, very likely, hurting it. Examine the existing culture closely, with a view to identifying constructive and destructive contributions.

For the purpose of this book, "culture" is defined as the firm's shared traditions, philosophy, values, style, policies, and behavior patterns. Mission Statements, compensation mechanisms, social priori-

65

ties, and business decisions are shaped by culture; a well- understood corporate culture guides people in behavioral choices.

A merit-based culture that instills enthusiasm and commitment, fosters a sense of identity with the firm, and is guided by ethical values makes it easier for all concerned to make decisions consistent with the firm's Mission.

Lack of unity and disagreements about the firm's Mission and values lead only to confusion; lack of shared clarity means that people don't have the benefit of cultural guidance in their day-to-day activities and decision making, exacerbating inefficiencies and lowering productivity. Employees concerned with making an incorrect decision may pay more attention to the letter of the law than to the spirit of the law.

Example: Early in my career, I joined a small company which had been founded by several former professors. The firm's mission was heavily influenced by its revered founders, who embraced a mission of scholarly exploration above all else. This culture served the firm well; its clients came to see it as a trusted and highly cerebral advisor. Several years after I joined, the firm was acquired by a large corporation. It soon became clear that people in other parts of the corporation viewed our scholarly approach as overly arrogant. It became evident that a number of people, including top managers within the corporate parent, wanted to see us fail. Needless to say, with these conflicting priorities, the wish became a self-fulfilling prophecy. The lack of collaboration all but ensured that intended synergies were never realized. Over subsequent years, many of the scholarly types left the acquired unit, to the point that its culture and offerings became commoditized, and far removed from the special partner clients had appreciated in earlier years.

The corporate culture has much influence over a firm and its performance: it is critical that you understand the existing culture fully. Ask these questions:

- How is successful performance defined?

- How is performance rewarded?

- How are decisions made? How many people are involved, what are their roles, which units do they represent?

- Are there well-defined paper or electronic reports? Are verbal reports considered adequate? Are the formal and informal reporting systems mutually exclusive?

- How is risk tolerated? How is risk managed? By whom?

- What is the corporate Mission Statement?

- What are the corporate priorities?

- How does the firm view its role within the local community?

- What is the firm's lore? Are there any legends or special stories told about the firm's founders, history or management teams?

- Which traits or achievements are most celebrated in the firm?

Is the firm's culture cohesive? Does it consist of several subcultures, put together through acquisitions or corporate realignments rather than organic growth, which have created fractures and an "us-versus-them" attitude? If the culture is not cohesive, melding the parts into a smoothly-functioning whole will take time, patience and consistent effort.

Review Internal Systems, Processes and Controls

A solid review of internal systems, processes, and controls is a critical task; inadequate (or non-existent) procedures, policies, and checks and balances may be a significant source of current difficulties and/or may lead to future problems.

The absence of controls typically results in minor to mid-sized efficiency losses, but can lead to more serious, even devastating, outcomes: massive loss of records, damage to important assets, vandalism, large-scale fraud or theft, and even mortal danger to people within and outside the firm are all documented results of inadequate controls.

Clearly, it is critical that you audit the systems thoroughly, identify the shortcomings, issue policy statements and initiate a correction plan as soon as possible.

Policies, processes and controls over those processes are synonymous with information technology (IT) systems. There are few industries in which a company can compete well without some reliance on IT systems. Systems can be as simple and low-cost as a cheap e-mail solution or a free publicly available Internet search engine, or highly complex systems that cost hundreds of millions of dollars.

Regardless of the cost or the sophistication of your infrastructure, here are some important questions to ask when auditing systems and controls:

- Which basic tools (software, hardware) does the firm have?

- Are these sufficient? While the question is simple, arriving at an informed answer may be very challenging.

- Do these tools represent overkill? Are they more complex and costly than necessary?

- Is staff sufficiently skilled to maintain and extend existing systems to service the firm's needs, now and in the foreseeable future?

- Can the existing or desired capabilities be used to create an advantage in the marketplace over competitors?

The last point is worth emphasizing: effective internal systems can give you an advantage in the marketplace. A company with very efficient internal project management infrastructure can adapt the same tools and skills to deliver consulting services to clients; the efficiencies can mean deploying consultants with less downtime. This more efficient utilization of staff time makes each individual more productive; competitors who can't match this are at an immediate disadvantage, giving you the opportunity to expand operations at the competitor's expense.

With the boom in available IT solutions, many firms are struggling to adapt to an ever-changing world, in which all aspects of their business are continually affected by technology. Everything from inventory management, billing, product design, production, sales, marketing, client service, contracting, and so on, can be affected: the outcome can be either positive or negative.

Strive to discover which aspects of the business are affected positively, or negatively, by existing systems. You must then strive to leverage those areas where IT systems are contributing positively and, conversely, re-engineer or replace those systems contributing to reduced productivity.

Properly understood and utilized, IT systems can do wonderful things for a company, large or small. Lack of sufficient understanding of IT systems, however, can lead firms to either under- or over-invest. Both outcomes are bad. Embarking on an unnecessary project and/or ignoring a much-needed one translates quickly into wasted time and money. A symptom of insufficient understanding of information technology within the firm is too many, or too few, IT personnel.

Technology is a competitive necessity, so even if you don't like it, you can't ignore it. Using inferior technology puts any company at a competitive disadvantage. On the other hand, loading up on too much new hardware and software will skim off, or completely obliterate, your margins: there is no alternative to ensuring you have the right equipment and staff with the right mix of skills.

The frustration associated with inefficiency and wastefulness can alienate staff and lower morale. You must ascertain whether inadequate systems are keeping staff up at night, whether systems are unstable and unreliable. Is senior management perceived as having its IT act together? Staff members recognize the importance of IT systems and have arrived at their own conclusions; when existing systems or known, future IT plans are inadequate, the staff will see the firm's competitiveness slipping away and attrition rates will increase.

Frustration is prevalent in troubled firms; the IT infrastructure and the IT staff are common targets of that frustration. Sometimes, the IT staff deserves criticism, but they usually can't be held accountable for *all* dysfunction; judge the IT systems and personnel fairly.

You may elect to outsource maintenance of certain systems to increase efficiencies or reduce costs; however, you must ensure your firm retains sufficient expertise to handle its needs, especially in a time of crisis. When you are deciding whether to outsource any critical functions, weigh the risks carefully: an outsourcing decision that appears to save money in the near-term may turn out to be far more costly if you are giving up control of mission-critical infrastructure.

Assessing IT systems requires skills and experience: ideally, you will bring sufficient knowledge to the table personally. The next best thing to having the knowledge yourself is to create a team with the depth to advise you: an organization dependent on a single expert in any department is likely to be at a disadvantage when one person has too much power and may constrain your decision-making. Every executive should be at least IT literate.

Below is a partial list of processes to investigate: evaluate the existing capabilities against a desired Best Practice. Examine the incentives in place: are these aligning people's personal interests with continuing searches for synergies and efficiencies in existing, as well as new, systems?

Client Relationship Management (CRM)

Timely information about client preferences, requirements, past habits, and decision-making processes is critical to every business. Managing client information can create competitive advantage or disadvantage. Some firms expend little on client information management, quite literally keeping their sketchy records on the backs of envelopes, while others invest heavily in systems and procedures that capture valuable information.

Ailing firms often suffer from deficient client management systems, and it always shows: client requests go unanswered, important communications to clients don't reach their intended destinations, and opportunities for additional sales are lost. When, inevitably, key staff leaves the firm, critical information leaves with them. Well-prepared firms document information thoroughly, and nothing falls through the cracks. Staff members don't forget to follow-up with an expectant client or prospect; even with the inevitable employee turnover, the incoming person can access the relevant records, identify loose ends and continue the work seamlessly. Detailed client records also allow proactive data mining for marketing, as well as decision-making for better service.

Some questions to address:

- Are your client systems capturing all the information you need?

- Are your systems functioning to your satisfaction?

- Can staff find information in a timely fashion?

- Does staff have the tools to analyze the information properly?

- Are there mechanisms in place to ensure that any insight gained from analysis is relayed successfully to those who need to know it?

Billing

Finding new clients to stimulate cash flow is challenging enough; the last headache you need is worrying about tracking payments from existing clients. Surprisingly, however, many troubled companies have poor processes in place; the scramble to *track* cash flow consumes resources which are far better concentrated on *stimulating* it.

Malfunctioning systems can damage your firm's professional image. Imagine calling a client to ask for their payment, only to have them inform you that, "according to our systems, you cashed our check four weeks ago, and why don't you know that?!"

As bizarre as it may seem, some companies can't easily determine whether they've received payments, how much they've received, or whether there are balances owed; the names of their contacts within client institutions, which products their clients are using, are similarly mysterious.

Have you inherited these deficiencies?

Anyone who has been in business long enough has witnessed many—or all of these situations—and knows this isn't good business practice. Don't tolerate it in your institution!

Usually, systems dysfunction will be brought to your attention quite quickly by a frustrated employee seeking your help; the relationship manager or sales associate who suffered embarrassment when the client angrily demanded to know why a new bill has been received when the check has already been cashed, or why the amount on the bill is completely wrong, would be remiss in not speaking up.

Find out why the records are wrong. Some relevant questions:

- Are finance systems performing properly?

- When problems arise, do the people responsible respond quickly and accurately?

- Is information taken from multiple systems without accurate reconciliation?

- Are multiple people entering overlapping information into multiple systems, thereby introducing inconsistencies?

- Who has authority to access and/or amend records? Should authority be restricted or expanded?

Contracting

There are good contracts and there are bad contracts: the good ones protect the firm's interests, the bad ones don't. In the worst cases, poorly written contracts leave you open to litigation and legal costs. The best time to make sure a contract is a good one is before it leaves the office: after all parties have affixed their signatures is not a good time to request changes.

When you first arrive on the job, examine important contracts to gain a more precise understanding of the agreements with clients, suppliers, partners, and staff. Wherever you identify problems, trace them to the source and correct processes as needed to ensure problems don't recur.

One of your early challenges will be to evaluate your legal advisors' performance. Advisors who prolong the contracting process just to justify their own existence (and/or to inflate their bills) or insist on drawing out contract negotiations or adding inane revisions will harm your professional image: yes, it's possible to lose a deal in the contract stage, so don't waste any time. Ensure that your contracting capability reliably protects the company's interests, and does so in a professional, comprehensive, and efficient manner.

It's acceptable to occasionally compromise on certain legal clauses when there is real strategic benefit; it is not acceptable to get caught up in a never-ending spiral of compromises just to get some business.

Some compromises are misleadingly justified as "strategically important." The point here is that not every deal can be strategic; if your sales people keep using that line to justify bad deals that expose the firm to risks, the sales people either don't understand the business, or they are unable to negotiate effectively.

Useful questions to ask:

- Do sales people seem to negotiate good deals?

- Is contracting considered a bottleneck? Does it cause delays in executing business and cause the firm to miss opportunities?

- Does it appear that contract sign-off takes an inordinate amount of time?

- Does legal staff get along well with everyone else, especially those in the sales and business development function?

- Have there been problems in the past with contracts failing to provide the intended protections?

- Are clients or partners able to exit from contractual agreements by exploiting previously-unidentified loopholes?

Example: Years ago I was charged with managing the business development activities of a large and bureaucratic company. On one particular occasion we made good progress with a prospect, and ultimately provided to them our standard contract. Predictably, they responded with suggested revisions. We duly handed these off to our contracting department, which was responsible for assessing our ability to meet the client's contractual demands, and to coordinate internally with our legal department to ensure our liabilities in all cases were acceptable.

Days turned into weeks. The relationship manager became annoyed, then concerned, and finally angry. Before the contracting phase, the deal had a good rhythm. We'd made a good first impression, followed up with successful demonstrations and subsequently with product literature that was well-received. The rapport was good at junior and senior levels. But then, the contract delays disrupted all the goodwill. The client began to question whether we were truly interested in their business.

I inquired with the contracting department and was told dismissively that the delay was due to back log in the legal department. After a few more days we followed up directly with one of the lawyers, who expressed surprise at the earlier explanation, as she was quite certain the paperwork had not yet arrived in her department. Armed with this information, we were able to extract an acknowledgement from the contracts department that the original paperwork, was, in fact, still in their care, and had not been forwarded!

The paperwork was quickly processed, and the deal was completed, after a number of us provided sincere apologies to the client.

Behind the scenes, I sought an explanation for the delays, and was shocked to find that the paperwork had been deliberately withheld by a middle manager in the contracts department. He didn't want to provide quick turnaround because, as he put it, "We can't afford to spoil them [our salespeople] too much with quick turnarounds, because that will make them impossible to deal with when we do have delays."

The response was so surprising and the manager so convinced he was serving the firm's long-term interests that my anger quickly dissipated. I found myself explaining that we (collectively, the firm), were there to serve clients' needs. Slow response times that negatively affected prospects and clients could never be justified, and certainly not as a by-product of "punishing" our own sales force.

Human Resource Processes

Many troubled firms suffer from inadequate Human Resource (HR) processes. Small companies may lack routines and systems completely; but, even large firms with dedicated human resource departments can manifest deficiencies. Widespread deficiencies are symptoms of poor management at the very top of an organization. Managers who love to tout their commitment to people, but whose actions are inconsistent with their statements, are among the most destructive human liabilities.

Human resources departments are often viewed as cost centers, and are not given sufficient resources to create or maintain critical infrastructure to track and manage benefits, handle recruitment, evaluate employee performance, and protect the firm from employee lawsuits. Human resource functions are needed to tend to your battle-scarred staff and support recruitment of the very people who will help you to turn the firm's fortunes around.

The message here is very simple: if you are committed to people, and to the firm's character and morale, there is no substitute for processes to support the efforts of your skilled human resource staff.

Questions you should ask:

- What policies and procedures are in place for managing existing staff and bringing in new people?

- What training resources are available for new recruits?

- Are there solid mechanisms for caring for people's needs—sick leave, bereavement or maternity leave, retraining, business travel reimbursement? Is the human resources staff knowledgeable and helpful?

- Are there processes in place to consistently measure people's contributions, performance, and personal growth?

- Do policies and processes encourage high quality, two-way communication among employees and their managers? For example, are managers required to meet one-on-one with employees on a monthly or quarterly basis, and provide feedback in a casual and non-threatening environment?

Payroll

Paying staff and suppliers on time is a non-negotiable requirement for any company. Astoundingly, many firms (of various sizes) do not make payments in timely fashion. Sometimes, there is a tendency to excuse small firms, especially struggling ones, for late payments; some large firms make payments late, simply because they can get away with it—arguably a form of bullying. It may appear to make sense in the near term, but "what goes around comes around." If you don't treat others well, when you need them they are much more likely to abandon you.

If a manager dismisses staff frustrations about late paychecks or travel expense reimbursements, you must explain to that manager *firmly* that timely compensation is not only a sensitive matter, it is a legal requirement for employers. The earlier discussion of the drivers of human behavior bears repeating: Don't mess with the Key Drivers of Human Behavior (respect, compensation, upward mobility, clarity, dignity)!

Example: Here's a disturbingly common example from one large corporation's reimbursement process. The firm, employing tens of thousands of people around the globe, required employees to use personal credit cards to make purchases while traveling, and then to request reimbursement by electronically filing expense reports.

The complete process was probably no more cumbersome than many: an employee incurs the charge for an airplane ticket, hotel room and or meal, typically settling the bill with a personal card. The employee would then submit an electronic report of all monthly expenses using the firm's intranet site. The report would then be routed electronically to the employee's immediate manager, who would sign off electronically, then be forwarded to the next manager in the chain, requiring her signoff, then proceed to the next level, requiring an executive's signature.

At each required approval level, if a report rested unapproved in a manager's inbox for two weeks, it would be returned to the submitter automatically. Resubmission would then be required, through the entire chain of command, gathering appropriate signoffs at each level, before moving on to the next.

Within this process one hapless employee submitted a report for $12,000, a reasonably common total for a trip involving international travel (business class flights and a decent hotel). The report was approved by the first manager, but was bounced back because the second manager was away from the office, and unable to approve it in the two-week window.

The report was resubmitted immediately by the surprised employee, clearing the first manager as before, then a few days later the second manager. But then, after a two-week delay, it was returned automatically to the employee. The report was quickly resubmitted, with great urgency by the employee, who now realized she was getting charged interest by her credit card company. The report was delayed for a week because the immediate manager was on a business trip, and then finally clearing that hurdle, cleared the next one quickly as well.

It then set for two weeks in the executive's inbox, and was again bounced back to the now-seething employee. To cut an agonizing story short, the report was finally signed off, after 4 months!

A number of useful observations may be gleaned from this example:

First, the system was too smart for itself. The two-week automatic bounce-back routine was in place to ensure that no report would fall through the cracks, setting for months on end in a manager's inbox without anyone noticing. Instead, the procedure contributed to significant delays.

Second, the firm exhibited extreme bureaucracy. Couldn't anyone have circumvented the system and obtained approval outside it for the increasingly-frustrated employee?

Third, the employee was effectively, and unfairly, being asked to subsidize the expenses of an international conglomerate.

Fourth, the employee's anxiety went through the roof. She was concerned about being blamed for the delays, suffering damage to her personal credit rating, not receiving any reimbursement, and possibly having to cover the interest payments herself.

Her anger at management and the lingering resentment were significant. End note: when the firm finally did approve reimbursement, it did agree to cover the interest payments. It was able to do so in record time. It only took three months!

If a manager truly believes that timely payments are of little importance to staff, the staff will lose trust in him, and the firm as well. One employee's loss of trust is ominous; widespread loss of trust can be devastating, particularly when employees complain to the local version of the Wage and Hours Division.

Despite the importance of timely, equitable compensation, far too many managers seem to convince themselves that their magnetic charisma keeps the staff engaged and motivated, and their verbal assurances will calm everyone and get them back to work productively. This works on rare occasions, is sustainable for a short-term only, and must be in combination with an articulated plan for ending the austerity measure.

Managers are paid more, and may be less likely to have real-world financial challenges faced by more junior staff. Yes, having to wait a month for reimbursement of $500 in travel expenses can be a problem! The amount may seem inconsequential to the manager, but the staff member's perspective may be far different.

Getting that monthly salary on time is usually the only way to pay the mortgage, car payment, and children's tuition: very few independently wealthy individuals work in junior staff positions.

Never underestimate the importance of paying people on time: whether they need money urgently or not is irrelevant; the firm is obligated by law to pay them in timely fashion.

Clearly, your payroll system must be robust. Ask people at various levels whether the relevant systems work adequately from their perspective. If you pick up any indication that there are issues with existing processes, investigate until you get to the bottom of the issue. Important questions to ask include:

- Are the processes manual and subject to human error?

- Are they too complex and confusing, causing delays and errors?

- Is there anything about the firm's incoming cash flow that may cause late payments to staff?

The latter is especially likely in a turnaround situation; the firm may be facing a serious cash imbalance, which often indicates a much more serious cash flow problem.

Time Tracking

One of the keys to efficiency is staff working full days. Many firms track people's time formally. People who are paid an hourly wage rather than a salary may "punch-in" (insert a paper card into a time clock which stamps the date and exact time of arrival or departure). Punching-in may ensure that people are in the office or production facility, but it doesn't ensure they are working productively: measure employee productivity by volume and quality of output.

In other cases it's necessary to track and allocate people's time to specific projects or contracts; advisory and consulting services fall into this category. It's necessary to identify billable and non-billable hours for each employee; billable projects are those clients pay for directly and are the primary source of income for such firms.

Increasing billable hours means healthier revenues and margins. Tracking hours consistently and accurately ensures that the workloads and available staff tally. Forecasting staff availability for consulting projects is very difficult without accurate data; if there are more projects than current staff can do, recruiting, hiring and training people is necessary; if there is not enough work, staff will be idle.

To measure relative productivity, managers can compare the number of hours it takes different teams and individuals to complete similar projects.

A consulting company can have brilliant staff members, all well-intentioned, experienced, and good with clients; however, if their time management system is less than perfect, they will lose efficiency and profitability. In extreme cases, frustration, resentment, less respect for management, and departures result.

Staff members often resent time tracking systems, for several reasons: one is that the systems are not very user-friendly; another is that time tracking may be interpreted as a signal of management's distrust of staff. Some who are forced to report their time feel unjustly humiliated.

Important questions to ask include:

- Do existing systems track time accurately?

- Is time allocated properly to individual projects?

- Does time tracking create an advantage or disadvantage?

- How does the staff feel about the system used to track their time?

Know Your Partners

For the purposes of this book, a partnership is any agreement struck between the firm in question, and some other (non-client) entity, which may be an individual or a corporation. Typical partner functions include product distribution, advertising and marketing, alternative production facilities, or information technology outsourcing.

There are many considerations for choosing and retaining partners. There is no perfect relationship; inevitably, competitive issues, loss of sovereignty, security of proprietary information, etc., will arise.

For example, do you have any partners who come between you and your clients? This means that you are in the background, and the meaningful client relationships are actually held by your partner: this can be dangerous because, conceivably, your partner can find a replacement for you, or take on your role in servicing the client. Since the partner in this situation owns the client relationship, you would have little advance warning of such developments.

Large partners bring useful clout and brand name, as well as many resources. Generally, they have more to lose by cheating and may be expected to respect the letter of the law and your contracts. Don't underestimate the possibility, however, that even blue-chip firms may bend the rules or the law to get what they want.

A large partner's participation may be crucial to your success, but it may also wield great power over your fate; like it or not, you may become overly dependent on it.

Smaller partners tend to have fewer other partners and a less diverse clientele, and are more likely to be dependent on a single major client or partner. Furthermore, their businesses are less established and more volatile.

Generally, small partners are less likely to dominate you: but, in relative terms, they have less to lose and more to gain by bending the rules. They are more likely to renege on a partnership if, for example, they feel some other entity has more to offer them: the relative benefits of securing significant new income from the new partner are greater than potential reputation loss for their as-yet un-established business.

Furthermore, being small, they are less likely to be perceived as a threat by the jilted partner, more likely to have represented marginal business in relative terms, and therefore less likely to face legal action.

Smaller partners are generally more likely to fail than more established organizations; if any of your critical processes depend on partners, you can't afford to have them suddenly fail and leave you unsupported.

Take the time to understand your firm's external relationships; analyze your partners' capabilities, contributions, and deficiencies. Qualify potential partners early on, and validate any joint effort before significant expenditure of resources.

Answer these questions for each relationship:

- Is the relationship adding value? Is it a one-sided arrangement? Is the partner pulling its own weight? Is your firm doing its share?

- How responsive is the partner? Is there a track record, and if so, is it positive or negative?

- Is there more to be done together, more synergies to be identified and realized?

- Is this the right partner? Does it bring complementary skills and a constructive attitude to the table?

- Is it possible that the partner has a malicious agenda? Could it be cooperating merely to gain knowledge of your processes, clients, suppliers, expertise? Could it turn this against you? How much legal protection do you have against such eventualities? What risks do these possible outcomes represent?

- Is the contractual arrangement between you fair and sound? Do the contracts reflect your understanding of the relationship? Is the partner's understanding consistent, or conflicting, with yours?

- Is there a clear understanding of where each party's responsibilities begin and end? Loose contract language can make it difficult to clearly delineate the precise boundaries.

- Do you have a clear articulation of the joint Value Proposition of the partnership? (Value Propositions are explained in Chapter 7.) Just as each of your own initiatives must have a sound Value Proposition, a partnership must be grounded in a solid Value Proposition. What can you offer jointly that is unique, and difficult or impossible for you or competitors to provide otherwise?

- Do you have exclusive arrangements with the partner? This could prove advantageous or disadvantageous. You want to restrict the partner, yet keep your own options as open as possible; however, a fair agreement may require that you give up some flexibility if you realistically expect to restrict your partner's.

- Is there any logic to deepening the relationship, possibly through an equity stake or outright acquisition? How consistent is the partner's culture with yours?

- Does pursuing this partner allow you to progress with your strategy, or are you in danger of being dragged off-course by the partner? Determine your strategy; do not allow others to dictate it.

Be aware there are often political issues around partnerships; some partnerships are in place merely because the idea pleases a senior member of the organization. Is there cronyism at play? Is it possible that the arrangement is in place for non-economic reasons?

Make sure you personally meet the important partners (if logistically possible, meet all of them). Partners can be an effective extension of your company; it's wise to gain a complete understanding of the potential synergies. Some partnerships are a tremendous drain on resources, including management time and focus; in the long run, the value destroyed may exceed the value gained.

Example: I once inherited a distribution partner when I was given a product management role. The relationship had been in place for years, and it quickly became apparent that no one had given it much thought since its creation; very few units of our offerings had been sold by this partner in recent memory.

Upon reading the legal agreement governing the relationship, I discovered that our firm was paying the distributor fifty percent of all revenue for distributing our products. This hefty amount was far higher than industry norms, and the partner was also distributing competitors' product. In other words, we were paying a lot and we weren't even getting the benefit of exclusivity for our offerings.

A meeting was arranged with a senior executive at the partner organization, and following a very quick conversation, he agreed to revise the terms, giving us exclusivity, and promised to provide a more meaningful sales effort. By year-end, revenue had doubled. All it took was a close look at the agreement, and a quick conversation with the partner.

Openness with a partner will always appreciated, but there are situations in which you may choose to be more tight-lipped: if your research indicates your partner is playing two sides, possibly getting too close to one of your competitors, or even on the verge of becoming a direct competitor, for example.

Concern that your proprietary information (products, strategy) may filter through to the competition is real and you should be careful about revealing such information.

If walking away from a partnership will leave a gaping hole in your processes, consider lining up other more appropriate partners first to ensure a smooth transition.

Learn lessons from the past and insist on specific contract language requiring the partner to live up to their obligations. In addition to, or within the contracts, include detailed Service Level Agreements (SLAs), describing each party's responsibilities and mechanisms for dispute resolution. SLAs may also be used within a company, put in place between business units to document the mutual responsibilities of the parties; the main difference is that there is no legal recourse; one unit can't realistically sue a sister unit. There is, however, benefit to explicitly outlining accountability.

Some prudent content to include in contracts:

- If the partner is responsible for client support, but fails to be responsive, clauses setting out the penalties, ranging from your firm receiving a higher proportion of revenues, to voiding the agreement entirely.

- If a supplier is consistently late providing inputs to your processes, the price you pay per unit could drop.

- If a development partner drags its feet on joint research obligations, patent ownership may change hands.

Do not ignore the possibility that your firm is responsible for the dysfunction. This is especially likely given your firm's internal problems. If your investigations lead to this conclusion and you wish to continue the partnership, an apology or at least acknowledgement of past failures may rebuild some trust and pave a new path to mutual success. Keep in mind that, under these circumstances, your partner's staff will legitimately be frustrated and possibly angry. Give them an opportunity to vent and make a note of their specific concerns. Thereafter, SLAs may keep your own people disciplined to deliver your share of the partnership responsibilities.

Mechanisms such as SLAs are the minimum required by many companies; if the partner is aware of your firm's distressed status, other assurances that your firm will be a going concern long enough to deliver on promises and pay your bills may be required. Suppliers will demand payment on less accommodating terms, and may not allow your company much credit, if at all.

In some cases you may discover that the partnership is underutilized and that the relationship can be expanded; advantages include more opportunities for collaboration, avoiding the unknowns of approaching a new partner and building relationships from scratch. The disadvantage of moving to fewer partners is increasing your concentration risk: consolidating all your suppliers or distribution channels into just one opens your company to a much greater downside if the now-exclusive partner suddenly isn't there for you. The partner may be acquired, run into financial difficulties, or decide that it does not want you as a strategic partner.

One way to reduce the risks of high dependency on a partner, and simultaneously share more in the joint success, is an equity stake in the partner, or giving a stake in your company to the partner. Acquisition or sale decisions are complex and require due diligence. There is significant danger of getting distracted from fixing your own company first; many firms have turned to acquisitions as a panacea for their problems. The vast majority of such acquisitions ends in failure; do not be seduced into believing that buying another entity will magically rid your ailing firm of all its deficiencies.

Know Your Offerings

"Offerings" are products and services your firm sells to clients. Offerings must have a solid Value Proposition, be compelling as a stand-alone (sold as an individual solution) or in combination with other offerings (as a suite of solutions).

Having the right number of the right products that reflect the core business of the company is optimal; however, shifting markets, customer preferences, and the speed of technological improvements conspire to defeat the best-laid Business Plans.

Companies with too many or too few products, poorly targeted products, or products on the verge of obsolescence are clearly disadvantaged in the marketplace:

- Products must reflect the company's core business(es);

- Too many products increase support and maintenance costs, internally and externally;

- Too many products can create a lack of focus, particularly when the products are similar enough to cause confusion among sales staff and customers.

- Too few products limit the number of customers for whom the products are suited, limiting revenues, sales and growth opportunities.

Review all offerings individually; consider each product, tool, or service as it stands, ignoring potential synergies, comparing revenues to costs to measure profitability of each offering.

Be prepared for product managers' strident defense of their "babies," regardless of how well or poorly the product has performed; their enthusiasm is commendable, but must be tempered with the realities of the marketplace. Some offerings may have to be revised, combined with others, transferred to another department, sold, or discontinued.

Face the marketplace and internal concerns squarely: include product managers in reviewing market feedback, discussions and planning for immediate sales tactics and long-term sales strategy. Hearing the truth from *customers* about why a product is outdated, unfocused, or poorly positioned leaves the product manager with two basic choices: help fix the product, or be bypassed for the good of the company.

Ranking offerings by profitability is natural and useful; however, comparisons made with only short-term survival considerations can be misleading. Profitability measures are a function of timing: new products require investment, and expenses may be relatively high while revenues are still in the build-up stage. A year later, the picture may be very different, with higher revenues and lower expenses.

Conversely, technology underlying mature products may become outdated, requiring higher maintenance costs, and/or putting the firm at a disadvantage against newer products. Always evaluate products in terms of their life cycles.

Review products in light of the Business Plan. (Business Plans are described later in this chapter). Does each offering, individually and in suites, reflect the core business of the firm?

Example: *I once entered a new business unit which had four main offerings; three distinct products, and one service. Two of the products and the service were consistent with the firm's overall aims; the third product was clearly not connected in any way to the firm's overall Mission.*

The product manager acknowledged up-front that the product didn't fit, but it was the only one making money for the firm!

Successive management teams had decided to not "mess with success": they left it alone and focused on changes to the other three offerings.

If the firm's current Mission was up for discussion, re-orienting the Mission itself to match the successful product and reviewing and revising other offerings to be consistent with this new Mission vision made sense. If the firms' original Mission was unassailable, restoring focus was the first priority. We concluded the Mission Statement should stand; selling the inconsistent product and using the proceeds to invest in the smaller, more-focused offering suite proved how constrained past decision-making had been, because prior managers had relied on a "stop-gap" tactic that became their strategy by default.

Clearly, "misfit" offerings lead to distractions and inefficiencies.

When two or more products are so similar they undermine each other, one effectively "cannibalizes" revenue from others. Some highly innovative companies may use this technique purposefully, knowing new products will replace older ones, preserving revenues from mature products while winning clients from competitors or gaining access to new markets and growth with the new one.

Ailing firms, however, may find themselves constrained because none of the similar offerings can reach critical mass: clients confused by the similarity of the offerings may simply choose not to buy any.

Synergies among multiple offerings—when it is more compelling for a client to buy two or more of your offerings, rather than one from you and several others from other vendors—is a marketplace advantage for firms seeking to solidify customer loyalty with strong brands.

Identify sacred cows, mavericks, and strays among your offerings: head 'em up, move 'em out, and replace them with viable stocks-in-trade.

Know Your Clients

Client issues were not addressed first, but this is not an indication of the relative importance of reaching out to clients, understanding them, and servicing them properly. Many practitioners would argue that everything begins and ends with clients. If you don't make an effort to connect with clients and cater to their needs, you won't succeed. Quite simply, if you elect to ignore clients and leave them out of your information discovery process, your business will fail.

There are important reasons for reaching out to clients and prospects as soon as you arrive. *Make* the time to sit down with clients with a view to:

- Understanding what your group is doing right *or* wrong. As you listen to this information don't be defensive—take it all in constructively and incorporate it into evaluating the staff and managerial performance. You have an opportunity to collect invaluable feedback on people's strengths and weaknesses— take advantage of it.

- Learning exactly why certain clients chose you as a solution provider. This is important for establishing or refining your Value Propositions.

- Picking up some important information about the competition. Look for statements of comparison. Accept favorable feedback graciously, and probe for unfavorable comments or impressions. Find out what you should do differently and why.

- Making the difference on pending deals. Your presence, display of commitment, and personal credibility may help to win some important business early on, and set the stage for your turnaround. Nothing is more powerful than showing your stakeholders (senior management, the Board) a solid strategic sale.

The amount and quality of feedback you receive from client visits will depend on several factors:

- Your personality and approachability;

- The presence of others in the room. Clients may be disinclined to directly or indirectly criticize people who are present; create a private moment, possibly over a meal or a drink, with your counterpart in the client institution and gather the more private thoughts.

- The culture of the client institution. In some cultures it would be unthinkable to say anything negative in front of a client organization's senior executive, especially if the meeting is the first he has attended; the critical feedback may be given in subtle comments, or not stated directly. Ensure you have a staff member who understands the culture and language present and can help you interpret statements and behavior correctly.

- The quality of the relationship your firm has with the client institution. The deeper and more trusting the relationship, the more inclined the client will be to share thoughts and concerns openly and honestly.

Even if your initial visit leads to only tentative responses, you have taken a step forward in creating and maintaining open lines of communication. Repeated follow-up will help maintain and expand the discussions; eventually, the discussions will segue into a relationship. You want the client (or prospect) to see meetings with you as a desirable use of his time.

Repeated interaction with clients is critical in helping you and your firm understand clients' businesses. Your long-term strategies must anticipate a future which clients may not even be able to describe today.

While it's critical to hear outside opinions of what you are doing correctly or incorrectly as a firm, this does not mean embracing all the clients' requests and recommendations. Listen to clients and learn from them, but avoid allowing any one client or small subset of clients to drive your products and innovations.

Review Plans & Strategy

In addition to all the reviews discussed above, examine all Business Plans critically; every department, every level of the firm. Consider research and development, as well as acquisitions strategy.

Business Plans

Begin the process by having everyone, starting with the smallest functional groups or departments, review and present their detailed, existing plans. Each plan's details will (ideally) reflect that department's role. The plans should be subjected to scrutiny by all participants, including you; the head of each department should be able to demonstrate how each individual plan contributes to department-level plans, this time subject to scrutiny by fellow department heads. In turn, the managers of all the departments should then be able to tie all the group-level plans into a business unit-level plan. Continue with these critical reviews all the way to the top of the firm; your immediate reports will share their division-level plans with their peers, under your direct scrutiny.

Participants should be asking these critical questions at each level of investigation:

- Does the plan clearly articulate short- and long-term goals? Are these consistent with the firm's policies and over-all goals?

- Does the plan provide specific guidance for required staffing?

- Does the plan provide specific guidance for both short- and long-term investments?

- Do the long-term plans follow logically from the short-term plans?

- Does information technology play a role? Is the plan feasible in light of existing information technology resources? If not, does the plan outline future information technology needs?

- Does the plan take into account consumer/user tastes, and if relevant, potential shifts in those tastes?

- Does the plan take into account macroeconomic trends (for example, interest rate movements and shifts in the price of energy)?

- Does the plan take into account expected actions by competitors?

These questions are only a few of the potentially relevant questions. Encourage everyone to pursue any line of questioning that seems pertinent. The key is to ascertain whether a given plan is grounded in reality and whether it will achieve intended tactical or strategic objectives.

Lead and teach by example; participate personally whenever you can, especially wherever you suspect dysfunction. This review is a very useful mechanism for identifying weaknesses in your firm's preparation.

Do not allow unchallenged assumptions; think critically; make participants' contributions a factor in performance evaluations.

Ensure that everyone in the organization understands that these reviews are an educational process, and you are not attacking them personally. Already-anxious employees may assume that soon after a presentation, you (or their immediate manager) will fire them. Some anxiety helps people focus: too much anxiety is demoralizing; be mindful of individuals whose imaginations are taking them too far, affecting their own stability, and others'.

Example: I was in a company that created a new support unit by pulling together several hundred people from existing business units. For over two years, many people throughout the company believed there was a senior management conspiracy to create the special unit, then transfer into it all the weak or disliked people in the firm, and finally to formally disband the unit and fire everyone in it. The thinking was that disbanding the entire unit would legally allow management to fire all its members much more easily than it would to terminate them from their original positions. This long-lived paranoia hampered the firm significantly.

Anxiety will grip some people regardless of what you say; even if you've said all the right things, some people will remain unconvinced and assume you have ulterior motives. Sadly, the more often you reassure everyone that you are not looking for people to blame, the more anxious they become, convinced you plan to blame them. If you really are sincere, you will eventually earn their trust.

Getting hard facts and pushing past hidden agendas requires both macro-and micro-observation, starting at the 20,000-foot-level, and zooming down to the 2-inches-off-the-ground level.

Macro-level observations are your frame of reference for understanding how the parts and pieces make up the whole. Your first overview of the firm's current state and future plans will show you the most obvious trouble areas; look high and low and you will eventually find whatever there is to be found.

Some people may withhold information, particularly if they fear their work will not withstand close scrutiny. Despite this, you must continue your inquiries, set realistic goals, require people to perform competently, set high standards—and lead and manage by example.

When the right Business Plans are in place and being followed, you will have achieved an important milestone.

Research and Development (R&D) Plans

Research and Development (R&D) (paraphrasing the Organization for Economic Cooperation and Development's definition) is creative work undertaken systematically to increase the stock of knowledge, and use of that knowledge to devise new applications. Companies that surpass their competition by adding advanced features to current offerings, and/or developing new products, markets, technologies or processes have the advantage until the competition catches up.

Failure to innovate can be fatal for any company, especially in fields where innovation cycles are short; a firm that falls behind by just a few rounds may never be able to recover.

How do your firm's R&D expenditures compare to the competition's? Does the firm expend more, or less, than the industry norm (expenditure is often measured as a percent of revenue)?

When a firm runs into initial difficulties, its managers may elect to cut back on R&D investments. You should not be surprised to discover that your ailing firm has very little in the way of R&D activity or planning in place, because resources are spent on near-term survival.

Bring together those staff members who are knowledgeable about the firm's products and markets. Drawing on their experiences in the field, address these questions:

- Is the industry pursuing particular innovations which are "must haves" for any firm to compete effectively?

- How quickly will competitors be bringing their next generation of innovations to the market?

- How many innovation rounds is your firm behind the competition?

- Are there any research ideas which show great promise in practical implementations, but cannot be funded due to resource constraints?

- Is the firm pursuing any ideas that seem tangential to its long term objectives? In other words, is there reason to believe that the wrong research priorities are being pursued?

- Does the firm make good progress in research, but subsequently fail to implement the discoveries as successful commercial offerings?

The question of whether the firm's existing researchers are sufficiently talented and well-trained to contribute effectively and in timely fashion to future innovation is best asked in a more discreet forum of senior research executives and members of the human resources department.

Know Your Revenues

Obviously, revenues are crucial to every company; following the money is often the fastest way to determining causes of dysfunction.

Stakeholders, such as shareholders and Board members, often view revenue (revenue growth, in particular) as the most important indicator of the firm's success; from a financial management perspective, the firm can emerge from the turnaround once revenue growth outstrips expenditure growth.

A challenge for managers in turnaround situations is that there are people who may benefit, even if only in the short-term, from manipulating revenue numbers. These are typically people who fear their jobs will be lost if real forecasts are made known to senior management.

Before broadcasting revenue forecasts to stakeholders, you absolutely must know the true state of revenues: dig deep and examine the quality of the revenue pipeline closely. Your questioning should include:

- Is the revenue forecast real: does verifiable demand for your products justify the forecasts?

- Can the firm actually deliver the promised product or service (is it possible the solution was oversold)?

- Is the revenue sufficient? Will expenses realistically be sufficiently below revenues to ensure a healthy margin or net income?

Beware revenue forecasts containing probability weighted sums!

Most companies track potential revenue by listing the target institution or client, the nominal dollar amount of the contract, and a probability the business will be won.

It's common to find many opportunities with very low probabilities on such reports; salespeople will include such opportunities to create the impression that they are on track to meeting their sales goals; later, they can disown the deals lost as "long-shots."

When there are many low-, or very-low-probability opportunities, sums of probability-weighted revenue expectations across all these opportunities can still add up to significant (yet misleading) numbers.

For example, 20 opportunities with a potential contract value of $100,000 each still appear to translate to a significant amount of expected revenue at a 10% probability; the expected revenue adds up to $200,000—a significant amount for a small firm. In reality, there may be very little likelihood of closing any of these deals.

Insist on removing such entries from the decision-making process. When reviewing revenues, you could elect to impose a probability cutoff of say, 50 percent. This way, you will only be considering the more realistic, qualified leads and your forecasts will be more accurate.

Impose criteria to ensure the forecasted probabilities of closing sales are assessed consistently across business lines and regions; create a chart explaining clearly what it means to be at 40, 60, 80% probability.

- Forty percent could be assigned once a prospect has been qualified and has agreed to receive a proposal;

- 60% could be assigned once a presentation of the proposal has been made to senior decision-makers at the prospect institution;

- 80% could apply once the prospect asks to see an actual contract and indicates that your firm is the front-runner.

- 100% can only apply once the deal has been signed, sealed, and delivered.

- Alternatively, you may choose to assign 100% once the contract is signed, but keep in mind that it's still conceivable for the deal to turn sour, for the client to run into difficulties and cancel, and a whole slew of other potential complications.

- One way to prepare for such potential losses is to create a reserve account for cancelled or curtailed deals, missed payments, etc.

Ensure that an expense forecast properly accounts for all relevant costs; underestimating the full costs of a project or deliverable is a common pricing error.

Example: I was once in a firm with several offices around the globe. The North American office contained all the production facilities, while the satellite offices functioned primarily as sales centers.

Invariably, managers of these satellites calculated their profits as the difference between their revenues and their local expenses. The problem with this approach is that they completely (and conveniently) ignored the production costs, which were borne in North America.

Once taken into consideration, it turned out that the majority of the deals they had signed over a two-year period steadily lost the firm money. Thus, while they touted each new sale as a great victory, each deal, in fact, represented another nail in the firm's coffin.

An immediate step you can undertake in assessing the quality and realism of pipeline opportunities is to select a sample of prospects and instruct the relevant relationship manager to accompany you on visits to these prospects, to give you a sense of how real each opportunity is. Once you have sampled enough prospects, you will have a better sense of the accuracy of the forecast and the ability (or inclination) of particular relationship managers to make the correct call.

Familiarity with the firm's revenues and expenses must become second nature; when you can answer questions about either in your sleep, you have mastered them. If you agonize over the firm's financials to the point of having nightmares, you need a vacation.

Review External Factors

This section addresses forces which prevail now, or may emerge over time, in the broader economy or marketplace.

Traditional macroeconomic forces include prices of commodities such as oil and raw materials, interest and inflation rates and labor markets, as well as the generally-felt effects of recessions or expansions.

Relevant external forces include globalization trends and political environments; you can't control these factors, they are thrust upon you, so, you have to plan for them.

Despite your inability to change environmental factors, you ignore them at your peril, because they may have a tremendous impact on your plans and aspirations. You can't alter the actual factors, but you can make choices that protect you partially, or completely, from their effects.

It isn't possible to address each and every potential challenge that may arise; the most common and relevant factors are discussed below.

Macroeconomic Factors

Many books have addressed the effects of macroeconomics on business decisions; this brief discussion is an outline of some of the main challenges.

It should be clear that the traditional factors described above have significant effect on the success of your efforts. You could make a lot of good decisions within the context of the firm's internal woes, yet still be stymied overall due to commodity prices, scarcity of inputs into your critical processes, difficulty in hiring the right people during tight job markets, and so on. In fact, many a manager has lost heart when recounting all the uncertainties outside his control.

It's a big world and the combined effects of different permutations of these factors are numerous. A significant percentage of these are potentially fatal. There are no guarantees of success.

Forward-thinking managers identify key exposures to external factors and take action; minimum response to predictable, but not immediately probable risks—earthquakes, floods, bomb threats and kidnapped executives—is a written contingency plan, distributed to employees as well as managers. Showing employees the plans in place to protect them in a crisis, particularly when a manager or leader may not be available to make decisions, is a concrete demonstration of concern for their safety.

Many firms are significantly affected by the price of oil or other energy sources. Historically, large firms have been able to hedge energy costs in financial markets. Smaller firms had been unable to take advantage of such insurance due to its relative expense. Today, however, more derivative financial instruments are available, and competition has driven the price of such tools to a more accessible level for even smaller firms.

Innovation in financial markets has also made insurance or protection from many other risk exposures available, including greater accessibility to financial products for hedging against adverse interest and foreign exchange rate movements.

Example: Weather derivatives are an example of financial instruments designed to pay off when a particular region experiences rainfall above or below a certain threshold. Other instruments may pay the holder if more than some predetermined number of storms hit a certain defined region, or if temperatures are above or below certain averages over the course of a month.

You are wise to be aware of these tools, their applicability to your company's risks, and how to use them to best advantage.

Impact of Globalization

The environment in which your company operates is critical. Ignoring external trends and forces is equivalent to operating in a vacuum— clearly an imprudent response; our fast-moving, highly competitive world requires forethought and foresight from leaders in all areas, including government, business, and the military.

The defining external influence of the early 21st century may well be globalization. It's hardly possible for any business to operate without being influenced in some way by the increasingly global marketplace.

Globalization has been a factor for many decades, but its influence has accelerated dramatically in recent years as communications and transportation have leapt forward technologically. As noted by Thomas Friedman in his book, *The World is Flat: a Brief History of the Twenty-First Century*, the end of the Cold War brought down many barriers which had restricted globalization for decades. Since 1989, when the Berlin Wall came tumbling down, the world has been freed from bipolarization in which being in one camp (the Eastern bloc) meant being shut out completely from the other (the Western world). These historical restrictions applied in all matters political, but also influenced the world economy. Post-Cold War access to consumers and suppliers in formerly out-of-bounds regions has contributed to a mad dash of growth.

The whole world is competing for natural and human resources— suppliers, partners, and, of course, clients. You must have a keen awareness of the global setting within which your firm is placed.

Ignore the outside world at your peril!

Regulatory and Political Risk

Governments may affect your industry through two very different avenues: legislation or instability. Legislation refers to existing or future regulations imposed on your firm. Instability refers to dangers to your firm posed by a hostile government or other hostile political factions.

Legislation: Regulations may be imposed on you directly, or on your client base, or both. Some industries are more heavily regulated than others; regulations vary among countries, their provinces or states, counties, and cities. Governments vary with election cycles, the population's satisfaction with their elected representatives, and political expediencies, so regulation tends to ebb and flow with political climates.

Banking and finance are highly regulated. For firms in these industries, it is, therefore, critical to have a very deep understanding of past, present, and expected future regulatory moves. Predicting the direction the regulatory pendulum will swing is integral to strategic planning: Plan A for a more restrictive environment, Plan B for looser controls.

Instability: Do you have operations in countries that have endured, or are on the verge of, revolution, martial law being imposed, or outright anarchy? Do local political forces represent a danger to your staff? Political risk has led many firms to shut down operations in particular regions; many Western financial services firms pulled out of Southeast Asian countries when insurgencies picked up in their intensity a few years ago. Local corruption, kidnappings, intimidation tactics, and the general absence of the rule of law have forced similar actions in countries on the African and South American continents.

We often think of developing nations' politics as posing the greatest risks to our firms' ongoing operations and, sometimes, their very viability.

Interestingly, companies in democratic (and developed) nations may face significant political risk as well: one example is France, whose political system is influenced heavily by a population reluctant to let go of a decades-old social contract which effectively guarantees employment. This labor practice makes it very difficult for firms to shed employees, which, in turn, makes firms reluctant to hire.

This rigidity has historically been a significant obstacle to French firms' competitiveness—a fact which has caused them great damage as globalization has swept all corners of the world. Not long ago, hundreds of thousands of French protesters came out against a proposal to reduce rigid labor rules; experts expect current and future governments to generally respond as they have in the past—by giving in to these demands. While these rules persist, any firm with employees in France is affected, and potentially disadvantaged.

Political risk can be relevant in any country. Can you tell how your company's global operations may be affected? Do you get regular bulletins and reports from the U.S. State Department and its equivalent agencies in the countries where you operate? Do you have less formal, but timely, means of keeping tabs on local situations via newspapers, TV, radio and wire news services? Do you have contingency plans in place to safeguard employees and property if riots or other civil unrest erupts? Do you have native language speakers among your managers in foreign offices? Do you have reciprocal agreements with other companies for office and manufacturing space if your property is damaged?

PART THREE
PINPOINT CAUSES of DYSFUNCTION

CHAPTER 5
Determine Why the Firm Is Ailing

Your fund of knowledge gained from the reviews detailed in Chapter 4 is not yet sufficient capital to gamble on premature decisions. You have identified deficiencies within your firm, but are you sure they are the *real causes* of distress, not merely *symptoms*?

Every firm has weaknesses, but not all lead to distress; for example, you may identify a consistent lack of skills by members of your sales force. You could conclude that your most important priority is to invest in a sales force with appropriate skills. But what if the real cause of the firm's distress is that its products are completely outdated and cannot, at any price, challenge competing solutions? Had you spent all your capital on a shiny new sales force, you would still be left with nothing to sell.

It is critically important that your reviews be wide-ranging, but when you mobilize your scarce resources, focus on resolving the most immediate problems.

Your task is to determine which factors, combined with the weaknesses already identified, contribute directly (or indirectly) to your firm's dysfunction. The answer may be complex; avoid overly simplistic "fixes."

Unfortunately, you usually won't have the luxury of time to explore everything in complete detail; you will have to make assumptions to bridge the gaps in your knowledge; however, flawed assumptions based on mistaking a symptom for a cause will yield flawed decisions. Use the best, most current information available to you.

Repeat the "garbage in, garbage out," mantra often enough to remind yourself to take enough time for a "critical pause" before acting, but not so much you fail to act timely: defective inputs (assumptions) yield defective outputs (conclusions).

Example: I knew a company executive who used to periodically sit his management team down to compare his firm to the main competitor. Without fail, discussions turned to the question of how the competitor was able to be more productive—that is, generate roughly comparable revenue with fewer employees.

The subsequent discussion always ended up focusing on the hypothesis that the competing company had superior technology, allowing it to be more productive.

The implicit assumption made by this management team was that the quality of the average employee in their own firm was similar to that of the average employee in the competing firm. The group ignored the fact, which was brought to its attention on more than one occasion, that the competitor intentionally paid the highest salaries in the industry to ensure it attracted the best talent.

In light of this, a difference in employee productivity due to skills or talent was a distinct possibility. Yet, somehow, the management team refused to acknowledge this potential explanation for the productivity differences. Thus, the group regularly made an assumption it considered unassailable, and proceeded from that point with its analysis and (erroneous) conclusions. This example illustrates two important points: One, their assumption was flawed.

Two goes deeper: the group's leader did not ensure the integrity of the process. No objective effort was made to take a fresh look at the facts; complete and honest conversations were never permitted.

The causes of a firm's distress may be internal or external, business conditions thrust upon the firm, or related to human deficiencies. As comprehensive a list as could be mustered of these causes is presented in subsequent sections of this chapter. The classifications are not mutually exclusive.

Your task is to identify the specific causes most relevant for your firm; here is a sequence to follow:

- Use the lists provided in subsequent sections to identify the short list of causes you suspect are most relevant to the firm's dysfunction.

- Validate each item on the short list. That is, verify that the item is truly a cause, not a symptom, of the firm's distress.

- Gauge the relative impact each factor has in prolonging the distress; rank the factors in order of importance.

Once the most important factors have been identified, link each one to a responsible party (person or group of people) within the firm. "Responsible" means identifying those people assigned to correcting or controlling each factor. Choose them with great care, invest them with sufficient authority and resources to carry out their assignments effectively; do not hamper them with unwieldy constraints on their day-to-day efforts. Their input will figure prominently when the discussion turns to taking action to effect the turnaround.

One way to quickly identify some of the relevant factors is to create a questionnaire to distribute to management; consider distributing it to the entire firm. The questionnaire should seek comment on the factor(s) perceived to be at play in causing or propagating the firm's dysfunction. As a starting point, include the lists of factors from this chapter; leave plenty of space for spontaneous comment and factors you may not have considered.

Anonymity encourages candid responses; have someone who has no vested interest in the results collect and compile the results. Avoid any opportunity for the results to be contaminated or skewed—for better or worse—by personal motives.

Once the results are compiled, examine them; look carefully for patterns, obvious and subtle. Are some factors cited consistently? Are specific people or roles highlighted as contributing to the firm's successes, woes?

Spontaneous comments often reveal just how strongly the contributor feels: read them closely. When individuals or groups take credit for accomplishments—what is working—are they credible? Are some individuals or teams singled out for particular praise by others? *Are the statements themselves made in positive, or negative, terms?*

Be wary of misdirection. Is it possible a respondent is citing factors to take attention away from the true causes, because he fears repercussions? Do any comments appear to be politically motivated—shifting blame onto someone else, attempting to use someone as a scapegoat, or "get even" for perceived slights?

You may be thinking this approach reeks of fear of conspiracy; not necessarily: it is folly to fail to filter every response through your experience, business acumen, and intuition. A turnaround is highly stressful: people are afraid of losing their jobs, afraid they will not have a good reference if the firm closes; many will be angry, and will do whatever they can to survive, including blaming others.

It's up to you to scrutinize the company as if you're looking at it under a microscope; maintain that view until all the evidence has been unearthed, but remember to look up frequently and see the "big picture."

Do not jump to conclusions; do not let others reach premature or unsubstantiated conclusions, either.

Business Causes of Dysfunction

Entire books have already been written about each of these causes of business dysfunction; none of these are new ideas, but bear brief discussion.

High Financial Leverage: The firm's operations are reasonably healthy, but its financial leverage is too high. Leverage reflects the ratio of the firm's liabilities to its assets: the higher the indebtedness ratio, the higher the firm's interest payments on debt, and the greater the strain on the firm's finances.

If the firm's cash generation is volatile over even a few months, there may be insufficient cash to cover interest owed. Technically, at this stage creditors can step in and initiate legal proceedings: this ever-present threat can cause highly indebted (highly leveraged) firms to cut back on expenditures. These cutbacks may include slashing bonuses, eliminating perks, and deciding to forego otherwise-needed investments. The associated stress may also affect management's behavior, affecting staff morale in turn, creating more layers of anxiety.

Adverse Macroeconomic Environment: Factors no individual or company can control, such as unfavorable interest rates. When interest rates go up, the increased cost of funding ongoing operations can and does create a strain on many firms.

Higher interest rates may also make new investments appear less attractive or even impossible if the firm's interest payments are already precariously high; critically important new investments or ongoing ones are terminated, ultimately placing the firm at a disadvantage.

Resource Costs: When basic raw materials (oil, copper, steel, chemicals, etc.) costs go up, a firm's production costs can soar, causing extreme pressure on the firm's margins and competitiveness. While resource cost changes often apply to a whole industry, the more efficient companies are better able to survive, while the less efficient are the first to succumb to market pressures and ultimately fail.

Shifts in Business Cycles: Business cycles naturally consist of peaks and troughs. Depending on the industry, and the overall environment, the peaks and troughs may be separated by a period of five years, or twenty years.

When the downturn occurs, there is typically a decline in demand—and a glut of supply—due to built-up capacity that would have accompanied the previous upturn. Combined, excess inventory and declining demand lead to a price decline; as revenues erode, profits wane, and the firm may slip "into the red" (negative cash flow).

Competitive Landscape: Success is not an absolute measure of quality and innovation, but a relative measure of a firm's standing with respect to competitors.

As long as a firm is ahead of the competition, it has some advantages which can be leveraged in the marketplace to maintain an edge and be successful.

When the firm trails the competition, however, it must work extra hard to catch up. Competitive intensity depends on the industry, barriers to entry of additional competitors, and market saturation.

Geographic Over-extension: Many firms pursue growth by expanding geographically (nationally and/or internationally); the risk can be rewarded with new markets and lower production costs, but expansion can also endanger the firm.

The "tyranny of distance" includes higher logistical overhead expenses—transportation costs, expenses associated with mastering multiple cultures and regulatory regimes, the costs of additional office space, as well as communication challenges—which may complicate knowledge transfer and strategic planning.

In extreme cases, a firm may find its supply lines are over-extended, leading to costs that reduce competitiveness and profitability. Firms that cannot yet afford critical mass of personnel in all distant offices may frequently send scarce resources (experts) to provide local guidance and assistance. These frequent visits can prove very costly in financial terms, and may reduce the morale and productivity of over-extended, fatigued, home-sick travelers.

Target Market Shifts or Changes in Consumer Tastes: History is full of examples of firms which developed useful products but failed to identify shifts in market preferences and didn't adjust to changing needs. As the target market shifts, the firm must shift with it, or risk becoming obsolete. Depending on the firm's size, the nature of the market, and lead-time required for production changes, it may have more or less time to adjust.

The desktop computer industry measures product life cycles in months: producers must continuously deliver more powerful and useful machines; those who do not disappear quickly.

In contrast, the automobile industry has a longer adjustment period: the life cycle of a vehicle from design to industrial production may be four to six years. The result of American automakers missing (several) changing consumer trends, most recently from gas-guzzling SUVs to hybrid vehicles, is the same as in all other industries. While the American "Big 3" auto producers have clung desperately to their corporate lives, their steady competitive decline has led to significant distress, not just for their own companies, but their suppliers and the communities surrounding closed plants.

Government Regulations: Firms protected by government regulations may build entire franchises dependent on the existence of legislatively-created safe havens.

Highly regulated industries take advantage of barriers to entry to restrict the appearance of new competitors; firms tend to adapt to limited competition, and have little incentive to be "lean and mean." When regulatory protections are lifted, the firms are suddenly exposed to greater competition, and find themselves ill-equipped to make the necessary operational and psychological adjustments.

Perhaps the most dramatic recent example is the rating agency industry, which has been dominated for decades by Moody's Corporation, Standard & Poor's, and to a somewhat lesser extent, Fitch Ratings.

The barrier to entry leading to such dominance was the exclusive Nationally Recognized Statistical Rating Organization (NRSRO) designation provided by the Securities and Exchange Commission.

Since passage of the Credit Rating Agency Reform Act in 2006, the path to NRSRO status has become much more transparent and the designation much more accessible to other firms. This lays the groundwork for greater competition in the industry, presenting the three traditional market leaders with serious challenges.

Violence and War: Living in the "global village" with the 24-hour "if it bleeds it leads" genre of news coverage, we find ourselves overwhelmed by scenes of violence. Some of us are affected so profoundly that we lock our doors in the daytime, watch our children zealously and feel less and less safe in our neighborhoods. We have become fearful of others on the bus, look for subway vigilantes, and dread commuting lest we become victims of "road rage."

Sudden acts of violence—muggings, parking lot assaults, armed robbery, disgruntled employees "going postal," school shootings, riots, car-bombings, desecrating religious sites—whether aimed at your staff, or simply occurring near your company site, are frightening and distracting. Anxiety for family, friends, and colleagues' safety is a natural response to violence: who can think about accounting when the TV in the lunch room is showing pictures of burning buildings and wounded victims?

Prolonged states of war cause direct and indirect damage to private property and public infrastructure—buildings, factories, roads and bridges, railroads, shipping ports, telecommunications equipment, power and water supplies. Governments fall, public fire and police forces are overwhelmed, and fear for one's very life becomes real and immediate.

Terrorist attacks, whether launched by "home grown" or foreign-born criminals, cause suffering and despair beyond understanding; employees traumatized physically and/or mentally may be unable or unwilling to travel to certain locales, or to deliver products and services.

Ethnic conflict (local or distant) is a particularly insidious form of violence; it may affect the working relationships within the firm, most acutely when individuals who must work together identify with the warring parties. Global and domestic operations are at risk for highly disruptive tensions when even one employee harbors such negative traits and beliefs. Encouragingly, the farther away the conflict, the easier it is for employees to distance themselves from the hatred and violence and maintain productive relationships.

State- or National-Level Politics: (as distinguished from political machinations within the firm). Politics can favor or compromise a firm or industry. If a firm or industry becomes the target of political forces, it may be severely hampered. When public outcry over shortages, high prices, environmental damage, contaminated drugs, predatory or shoddy lending practices, unsafe cars or airplanes threatens a political administration's longevity, companies which have enjoyed the favorable regulatory environment may find themselves slipping out of favor as politicians flip-flop to avoid becoming the subject of public ire.

Natural Disasters: Every firm on the planet is subject to natural disasters: floods, fires, lightning, rain, hail, ice storms, hurricanes, tsunamis, cyclones, earthquakes, and perhaps the random asteroid. Employees and their families, as well as clients and suppliers, may be directly threatened or indirectly affected by disaster. Despite the existence of insurance products which can alleviate some of the damage, many firms realize too late that contingency plans are lacking and insurance protection is incomplete. In the worst case, the firm's most precious resource—its people—may suffer physical damage including death.

Fraud: Fraud is an ever-present danger. Countless firms, large and small, suffer losses due to embezzlement, "cooking the books," theft by deception or anything which, according to Barron's Educational Series, "embraces all the multifarious means which human ingenuity can devise to get an advantage over another. It includes all surprise, trick, cunning, dissembling and unfair ways by which another is cheated." (234 Federal Supplement 201, 203), cited in *Barron's Law Dictionary*, *3rd Ed*, (New York, Barron's Educational Series, 1991).

The most obvious direct damage is financial, but when individuals willing to compromise their own integrity and the trust of others are found in the company, remaining staff and management are more psychologically vulnerable; paranoia breeds further distrust. Highly reputable and wealthy firms have been irreparably damaged.

Several years ago, Barings Bank was taken under by massive losses resulting from rogue trading activities. Such spectacular failures are rare. Fraud often involves smaller amounts taken over longer periods, slowly bleeding away the firm's resources. Fraud may go unchecked for years, particularly when the thieves include management. Clever criminals may hide their illegal activities so well, internal and outside auditors may not discover the fraud.

The notion that fraud and corruption are ills which plague companies only in less-developed nations is false. Corporations in highly sophisticated economies are vulnerable as well; consider Enron (U.S.A.) and Parmalat (European Union).

Pension and Healthcare Liabilities: Once upon a time, companies provided healthcare and pension benefits to attract and retain good employees. Now, pension and healthcare costs are liabilities many firms are obligated to support under local laws, their corporate charters, and employment or labor contracts. These mounting costs squeeze firms' profit margins; small and large companies have found the costs unsupportable, prompting them to discontinue commercial insurance and self-fund, or simply discontinue the benefit altogether.

Union Demands: Unions often provide a united and powerful voice to workers who may otherwise be exploited or deprived of human rights. Unions that become inflexible in the face of global forces and local needs, however, can create significant rigidity, hampering a firm's ability to reinvent itself to remain viable and competitive.

Ideally, management and unions collaborate on constructive agreements to preserve or enhance the firm's competitiveness, safeguarding the majority of employees' jobs and futures.

Disadvantageous Technology Shifts or Failure to Invest in Technology: Corporate history is littered with products and services made obsolete by newer and/or better technology.

A handful of examples include: (a) the switch from vinyl records to cassette tapes and subsequently to silicon-based CD and DVD technology; (b) the switch from traditional brokerage services to significantly less expensive online brokers empowered by advances in communications technology and computerization; and (c) displacement of propeller-driven commercial aircraft by jet aircraft.

It would be easy to fill this entire book and several other volumes with such examples.

Inevitably, and frequently, existing products based on older technologies become obsolete and are discarded or bypassed. Any firm that fails to (a) either develop new technologies or at least recognize competitors' new technologies, and (b) embrace such new technologies—including reinventing itself when necessary—is, quite simply, doomed.

Reputation or Integrity Concerns: To realize long-term success a firm must honor the trust placed in it by consumers, suppliers, distributors, employees and investors. Many firms can survive economic downturns, shifts in consumer tastes and preferences, as well as tightening competition.

When a firm stumbles morally, however, it destroys trust with all market participants: competitors are sure to make the most of the opportunity by poaching staff, partners, and clients.

Citigroup's Senior Risk Officer, speaking at a 2006 forum in New York, discussed his perspective regarding the risk of reputation damage to a firm. Citigroup is one of the world's largest financial institutions, and the executive was charged with understanding, overseeing, and managing the firm's operational and financial risks. He explained that typical losses due to these risks may, as a matter of course, amount to *billions* of dollars annually!

Yet, he observed that even the slightest perception that the firm's integrity might be compromised would be far more damaging to its ability to attract investment capital, keep productive, competent managers and staff, maintain operations, and turn a profit.

The importance of reputation is summed up by Steven Fink, in an article for *Franchise Times*; he observes that "perception always trumps reality."

Lack of Diversification of Suppliers or Clients: When a firm relies heavily on just a handful of suppliers or clients, it has put all (or most of) its eggs in one basket.

Losing a supplier of critical raw materials or components can disrupt production, causing serious problems with creating products or delivering services.

Losing clients raises immediate and serious revenue implications: the firm may suddenly find itself unable to honor financial commitments;

lenders may be unwilling to refinance or extend loans—committing to a firm with a non-diversified clientele would not be prudent lending.

Thus, losing either a key client or supplier can be extremely damaging.

Lack of Risk Management Processes: The first rule of Risk Management is to know how your company works; the second rule is to know who to ask when you don't know.

While a firm may be on a reasonable footing, it will always be exposed to risks inherent to the business: operational, financial, political, legal, or reputational. A firm can be lucky and coast along, with reasonable success, without explicitly devising risk management policies and infrastructure.

But risk improperly understood will eventually cause damage to people, property, or public perception. Remember the axiom "Failure to plan is planning to fail."

Human Causes of Dysfunction

Philosophically speaking, people are at the heart of *every* problem: individual and group behavior (acts of commission) can reduce the firm's competitiveness, damage its prospects, and place it on an unhealthy path. When management denies, refuses, ignores or fails to recognize external forces and internal deficiencies, it commits acts of omission. In such cases, management "knows or should have known" risks were present.

The root of "ignorance" is "ignore," an action word: people tend to perceive acts of omission as indicative of incompetence.

If the failures stem from lack of skills or staff motivation, the logical question to ask management is why these deficiencies remained unaddressed. Since the "buck stops with management," criticisms for dysfunction must ultimately rest squarely on management's shoulders.

Understanding individual and group behaviors and characteristics is necessary to any enterprise: without humans, there is no enterprise. The Dirty Dozen Destructive Human Traits doubles as a list of the essential human causes of dysfunction in organizations.

Ineptitude: Lack of proper skills or experiences to perform one's job well. Why would a company have unskilled, inexperienced staff?

Poor recruiting, hiring, training, development and retention practices result from many causes:

- Lack of qualified human resources professionals;

- Poorly-planned and/or too-rapid growth;

- Using rigid seniority or other standards for deciding who should retain a position during business contractions;

- Failure to compensate people commensurate with the job requirements and the labor market; and

- Failure to terminate the employment of any individuals who do not contribute to the effectiveness and efficiency of the company.

The net effect is having people being paid for doing jobs poorly, or not at all. Funds are spent unproductively; the opportunity cost is real. Those same funds could be spent on people who do the job well, realizing a far more constructive outcome for the firm.

People classified as inept are usually not purposely setting out to damage the firm's competitiveness: they would probably be insulted at the thought that they are hurting the firm. Their productivity can be addressed and improved; most employees who are inept because of poor hiring and placement practices are under considerable stress because they cannot enjoy and take pride in their work; an opportunity for training or reassignment is a minimum requirement once the performance deficiencies are identified. Failure to remedy deficiencies, once identified, is inept management.

Absent-mindedness: Inability or unwillingness to focus. This can be a natural state for some people who simply don't care enough about work to focus on it sufficiently; the condition may be temporary distraction caused by events in an individual's personal life or health concerns.

We all deal with personal stresses and strains and, for the most part, manage to handle them. We are all at risk for being overwhelmed or distracted by responsibilities for children, spouses, aging parents, family illnesses, financial crises, moving, death of a loved one, divorce, or simple sleep deprivation.

Very common medical conditions can contribute to absent-mindedness: allergies to foods, pollens, animal dander, molds and fungi; uncontrolled diabetes, hypertension, anemia or a host of other illnesses. Side effects or interactions of prescription and/or over-the-counter or recreational drugs have been known to cause "brain fog."

Regardless of the cause, inattention contributes to accidents and re-duced productivity, as well as lowering co-workers' morale.

Disloyalty: Failure, by commission or omission, to support a team or company's efforts; undermining the team's success by being self-serving and failing to accept that they are part of a bigger picture.

Employee disloyalty is a natural reaction to the firm exhibiting dis-loyalty to staff. When a company slides from profitability to dysfunction, it's quite likely that staff perceives the crisis as managerial inattention or incompetence—disloyalty to the firm's Mission Statement.

Pride or Vanity: Excessive belief in one's own ability, achievements, potential; often accompanied by discounting the abilities of others.

Vain people generally resent constructive criticism; this limits their personal productivity.

One troubling extension of this trait is that such people may insist on broader responsibilities than they are able to handle. At the extreme, they engage in "empire-building," creating fiefdoms and reacting sharply to any perceived effort to diminish their power or authority. These "mini-empires" are often dysfunctional, with significant morale problems, damaging staff and productivity.

Envy: Desire for others' traits, status, abilities, or situation.

Envy may be directed internally at colleagues, or externally at partners, clients, or competitors.

Envy directed at colleagues can manifest in overt or subtle competition, efforts to undermine another, wasting resources and sapping momentum.

Envy directed outward is just as damaging: a staff member may perceive better opportunities in a competing firm or supplier; short of his departure, the constant yearning for "something better" is a distraction.

Gluttony: Desire to consume more than one's fair share of the firm's resources. This may appear to be the same as greed, but there is a subtle difference: greed can be defined as *hoarding*, while gluttony can be defined as *consuming*.

Gluttons are those who waste the firm's resources on themselves, choosing the most expensive modes of transport, accommodation and, perhaps most classically, lavish and expensive meals.

Lust: Exhibiting inappropriate attention towards colleagues. Some people do not control their intimate personal urges, creating an intimidating environment for their colleagues.

Failure to exercise appropriate control is defined as harassment of fellow employees: it is very damaging for all concerned, as it goes well beyond annoyance or distraction to affecting people's sense of security and dignity.

The mere perception of harassment can cause significant distrust and anxiety among employees and can be highly destructive to an organization; the atmosphere is negatively charged by such behavior, and the anger it causes among victims and observers who wonder why such behavior is allowed can explode in ugly accusations, lawsuits, and significant costs for financial settlements.

Anger: Aggression or resentment directed at others; seeking vengeance. Some people may bring a "chip on their shoulder" from a prior employer and react more intensely than necessary; others are simply more prone to aggressive outbursts, or consumed by envy which manifests in anger and resentment.

Anger is very intimidating to those who witness it; it creates anxiety and hampers teamwork. Management's failure to establish a more comfortable and safer working environment erodes trust in leadership.

Greed: Desire for material wealth or gain.

Greed isn't the most pleasant trait, but it may not necessarily be damaging to the firm if greedy people can be directed so that their material success helps the overall cause.

A commission-based salesperson can line his own pockets handsomely while doing the same for the firm as a whole. The problem arises when such people see their business environment as a "winner-take-all" game: when other people win, they lose, and vice versa. Such people often act to undermine colleagues; some even resent the revenue the company receives as the result of their efforts.

When dysfunctional people covet—or gain—power, greater issues may arise, as their dysfunction is thereafter projected directly onto a larger group of people, their direct reports.

Greedy employees are a challenge; greedy managers are a serious problem.

Laziness: Avoiding work; unlike ineptitude, which may not be intentional, laziness is a form of malice because it's purposeful.

Lazy people choose not to contribute. Offenders, knowing their behavior is unacceptable, often try to hide their lack of productivity by blaming others, or by engaging in illegal activity.

Laziness on the part of an employee causes an immediate and direct loss in productivity. Indirectly, other staff members also suffer productivity losses, become frustrated at the offender, and resent the additional work they must do to "get the job done."

Morale is sure to drop if management is not stepping in to remedy the situation.

Sense of Entitlement: Unreasonable assumption that one is owed something by the company.

Some people simply believe they are entitled to extended vacations, working from home, paid meals, business or first class travel, annual raises, guaranteed bonuses, and a Thanksgiving turkey.

If the "entitled" continue to agitate, or spread dissension among their peers in an effort to pressure management to change policies, management has choices, ranging from immediately acquiescing, which is bound to lead to a long, unhappy road to more demands and further drain on company resources, to standing firm and watching people leave.

Clearly, if the "entitled" choose to leave when unreasonable demands are denied, their departure relieves some of the tension and distraction.

Prejudice: An unfavorable opinion or feeling, formed prematurely.

For example, prejudiced employees may not share assignments fairly or logically with people they are biased against; they may refuse to work with particular colleagues; they may spread rumors about colleagues.

Such unfounded bias leads to poor performance in at least two ways: work is not allocated based on capability, and victim(s) are demoralized leading to additional loss of productivity.

Prejudice is especially harmful when it's a response to legally protected characteristics such as a victim's age, religion, gender, race or disability: in addition to the significant damage imposed on the victims, the firm may face very expensive legal defense fees and liability for multi-million dollar settlements when prejudice is allowed to continue as a matter of "pattern and practice."

When prejudice rears its ugly head due to ignorance, it may be addressed through education and feedback mechanisms from management and/or peers.

The Dirty Dozen are regrettable but not illegal. The thirteenth, intentional **Criminal Behavior,** *is* illegal. Deliberately sabotaging the firm, stealing firm resources—or both—are punishable in both civil and criminal courts.

Criminal behavior can have its roots in any of the Dirty Dozen behaviors; the culprit crosses a line from damaging behavior that is not intentionally malicious to premeditated action—theft, sabotage, vandalism, character assassination, harassment or assaulting others.

A company already suffering hardships is more vulnerable to such criminal behavior because it may lack the leadership and controls to identify and stop sabotage and theft.

The Ultimate Cause—Poor Leadership and Management

People are *always* at the heart of an ailing firm's problems. Individual junior staff members, however, usually are not responsible for poor performance of an entire firm (unless the group or firm is quite small and easily influenced by just one person); their low morale, poor skills, lack of direction, and poor performance is the direct consequence of senior staff failure and lack of executive leadership.

Thus, the real causes of dysfunction in an organization are poor leadership and poor management; failure to lead, failure to manage people, operations, and risks.

In contrast, recognizing and nurturing present and potential leaders is the essence of brilliant leadership; the top leaders/managers who seek talent in the ranks and unselfishly see to their development are contributing far beyond their own individual abilities and competences.

Nurturing leaders requires:

- Allowing them to take on new challenges, experiment with new ideas, and fail (within reasonable limits);

- Maintaining a tolerant and supportive atmosphere that allows individuals to learn from their mistakes;

- Broad exposure to many aspects of the company's sales, operations, planning and risk management functions;

- Inculcating the necessity for taking responsibility for one's own professional and personal development, including developing confidence, maturity, and resilience along with technical skills.

Good leaders and managers motivate and empower others, provide focus and clear priorities, communicate openly, make defensible decisions, and act honestly.

In contrast, consider the many ways poor leaders and managers can damage a company by either causing problems (commission) or propagating them (omission).

Poor Leaders or Managers:

- Attract the wrong types of people;

- Fail to empower others;

- Either micromanage or don't manage at all;

- Don't have and convey a vision, creating confusion about the firm's near-term and long-term goals;

- Make poor strategic decisions;

- Prioritize incorrectly;

- Don't make time for, or care about, the staff;

- Don't really know the business;

- Blame others or portray them in a bad light to other senior managers;

- Are afraid to make decisions;

- Are afraid to take risks;

- Play political games;

- Abuse perks;

- Act dishonestly.

These are all examples of poor skills or behaviors; some are more harmful than others. Making poor decisions, erring in setting priorities, and not knowing the business well enough are bad news for the company, but are not nearly as reprehensible or damaging as acting dishonestly and abusing perks.

Poor leaders and poor managers lose the trust of their staff; alienated staff reacts predictably—the best employees find employment elsewhere, leaving less-qualified people in critical jobs. Productivity declines, financial results suffer, and compensation and investments are cut back, leading to more staff departures, and the firm's performance spirals downward.

Identify which, if any, of your managers exhibit these damaging behaviors, and take action to remedy the situation—fast!

Don't be distracted by managers who point fingers at their staff, blaming them for all the company's ills. Those staff members' dysfunctional qualities are management's responsibility; the managers should be seeking to convert the inept to skilful, the undisciplined to disciplined, the disloyal to loyal, and the inexperienced to experienced.

When a team fails, leadership and management must accept their responsibility: if an immediate supervisor is failing, his manager has failed, the next manager up the line has failed—right up to the C-suite (The "C" in C-suite stands for "Chief," as in Chief Executive Officer, Chief Financial Officer, Chief Operating Officer).

PART FOUR
TAKE ACTION

Previous chapters urged you to undertake a comprehensive review of every imaginable aspect of the firm, including its people, operations, partners, clients, and business plans.

In particular, Chapter 5 recounted ineffective business practices and reiterated "people issues" common to dysfunctional firms. The stated conclusion of the chapter was that the ultimate cause of dysfunction is poor leadership and management.

Having identified the causes of the firm's problems, it's now time to address the actions that must be undertaken to achieve the turnaround.

Chapter 6 discusses how to deal with people successfully. Chapter 7 focuses on planning. Chapter 8 discusses action items designed to turn people around, including the need for a capable human resources function. Chapter 9 describes action items pertaining to turning the company around, addressing corporate culture, internal processes, partners, and clients. Chapter 10 discusses some inevitable hurdles along the path to a turnaround.

The chapters discussing evaluation and assessment precede the chapters on taking action for the sake of clarity; this does not, however, suggest that you can allow yourself to complete all performance evaluations and business function assessments before making any decisions.

Your first decision—taking the job—is already made: now, you are the leader in name; next, you must establish yourself as the leader-in-fact.

You will have to make some decisions very quickly and take decisive action to stanch the flow of red ink and the departures of the best employees, simultaneously demonstrating to employees that you are in charge and making constructive decisions.

CHAPTER 6
Deal With People Successfully
Using Eight Core Principles

Behavior is guided by those internal controls we label "conscience" or the "still small voice." Your success will hinge on the way you treat people; the way you treat people is a consequence of the strength of your character and the principles you follow. Very few people are fooled by hypocrisy, at least not for very long!

This chapter covers Eight Core Principles or Values. The first (fairly self-evident) five are addressed briefly: Honesty, Respect, Fairness, Quality, and Enthusiasm. More detail is provided for the remaining three: Communication, Leadership by Example, and Decisiveness. Plant these seeds early; nurture them over time by embracing them personally and instilling similar values throughout your organization.

Honesty

The most obvious meaning of "honesty" is the refusal to lie—to yourself, or to any other person. Lying of any sort, by deliberate statements or withholding relevant information, is intolerable anywhere in the organization.

Organizations with a hierarchy of authority (power) seem to generate particular forms of dishonesty. Some managers feel it's legitimate to withhold information from staff they judge as not having the "need to know." The firm's true financial performance, intended strategic direction changes, partnership and acquisition discussions, concerns of the Board, and other sensitive information should be closely held; however, people have to have enough information to make valid decisions.

Do not assume that you know what others "need to know," particularly when people seek explicit answers to pressing questions.

Honesty reduces uncertainty. An honest answer, even if unfavorable, is easier to digest than a lie; truthfulness is mandatory if you are to gain, and retain, people's trust and respect. Remember that you have come into a situation rife with uncertainty; people will view you with a mixture of fear, suspicion, and hope. You will have to allay their fears that you're the new "hatchet man," their suspicions that you are questioning them to gather evidence against them, and support their hope that you really are there to save the company, and their futures, with it.

Answer the questions people ask you: honesty is the first rule of communication; courtesy requires honesty; honesty is fundamental to the exercise of emotional intelligence. If you do not answer their questions, especially the tough ones, you are dodging the issue; you are not leading well, not managing effectively, and destroying the hope that motivates staff to give you, the new person, the benefit of the doubt.

Intelligent, sensitive people can sense deception; hiding important facts lead to no-win situations. Once people conclude they've been deceived, and you can offer no proof to the contrary, they are right to leave! When "word gets out" that honesty is not your policy, you will find replacing employees much harder, and the people willing to work in a company with a reputation for deceiving employees will not be the most-qualified candidates. Dishonesty limits your choices: the cover-up is nearly always more destructive than the "crime," and a sure way to delay emergence from distress. Worst case, you lose the opportunity altogether.

Bad news is inherent in a turnaround. Honest communication of bad news is in everyone's best interest: just make sure you tell them all the good news, too. The good news is the source of their hope and motivation to continue their efforts, sharpen their focus, and seek the vision.

A final thought about honesty is that it also applies to what you tell yourself. Honesty with oneself may seem simple, but is not always easy: introspection and evaluation of personal performance requires great courage. Discovering the same capacity for frailties of character as any other human being within ourselves is humbling.

Respect

Treat people respectfully: the highest ranking Executive Vice President down to the people at the bottom of the corporate "food chain" are human beings.

The first measure of respect is to purge your language (and insist that others follow your example) of derogatory and judgmental phrases such as references to hierarchy as a "food chain," or to junior staffers as "little people," "boy" and "girl."

Make your own list, starting with any label *you* find hurtful, distasteful, or denigrating; ask your family and friends for their "lists," and solicit feedback from employees, continuing to be mindful of how powerful words really are.

Constructive collaboration across all functions and levels is necessary in every firm. Collaboration comes from the heart. When people like their place of work, feel respected and appreciated regardless of their position or rank, they are effective and efficient.

Example: *I recall one occasion when I came to pitch products to a very well-known consulting company.*

The presentation room was full and the atmosphere was vibrant. One young woman sat in the middle of the room and was clearly the center of attention. Even before we started, it was clear that people enjoyed sparring with her verbally, and during the presentation she asked many questions.

She was clearly one of the high ranking, powerful, dynamic and charismatic business school graduate types, taking the world by storm. By the end of the session I felt we had really connected and I walked out of the room, elated at the thought that I had possibly made a million dollar sale.

Later, I found out she was the company's receptionist.

There are several points to this story: One, I jumped to conclusions, which is not a good thing to do. Two—and a far more important lesson—this company had a wonderful sense of camaraderie and inclusiveness. Their atmosphere of mutual respect allowed everyone to be involved and to feel a part of the team, regardless of how many years each had spent in school, their salaries, or particular function.

In other firms, the receptionist may have been ridiculed for asking a question. More likely, she would not have even been invited to join the meeting.

Since then, I have been forever striving for an inclusive atmosphere in my teams!

Leaders set the stage by taking action and making choices that make it clear to people you respect them and their needs.

Do you spend time on winning one more deal, or do you spend time instead on improving the internal payroll system so salespeople get paid their commissions on time, instead of having to wait for the finance department to find time to manually cut each check, perhaps stretching the process into several months?

It's easy to always go for the deal and rationalize the choice with a cliché such as "the customer always comes first." The first few times you say that, people may agree; but, as the months roll by people will begin to wonder whether their needs are on your priority list at all.

Within the context of choosing your people over potential clients, consider this radical idea: the client is *not* always right. Pleasing the client is *not* always the best move, especially if the alternative means losing good people. Commit to your people first: good people can always get more clients.

When people treat their seniors better than their juniors, it (depending upon the culture) can be a sign of elitism or arrogance, neither of which is consistent with respect. Set an example by referring to all staff members as "colleagues"; don't reserve the word just for professionals, while referring to administrative staff as "secretaries."

People in a distressed firm may treat each other with less respect simply because general frustration puts everyone on edge, causing resentments, reducing productivity, hurting the firm precisely when it can least afford the damage.

A troubled firm may seek to cut costs by reducing expenditures on some of the staff. Do you have catered meetings exclusively for professional staff, while administrative personnel are excluded? Is it more important to feed one type of staff member than another? Ironically, those usually fed at meetings are the ones who can most easily afford to feed themselves.

Furthermore, why would you exclude support staff members from meetings in the first place? If they know what you are trying to achieve, they are better positioned to provide support. Of course, not all meetings are relevant to everyone: the point is that too many managers effectively ignore the existence of support staff.

Example: *Many years ago, I was a graduate student, nervously trying to practice my thesis defense at the Wharton School of Business. To try to replicate the* *setting as much as possible, I entered the presentation room one evening and, speaking to the empty room, proceeded to do a dress rehearsal. About half-way through, I realized that a night custodian had entered quietly and had begun cleaning in the back. A few minutes later she sat down.*

When I got to the end of my rehearsed words, I stuck to the script and said, "Any questions?" I was about to begin collecting my notes when, to my astonishment, the woman slowly raised her hand. With my voice quavering, I pointed to her and said yes? She proceeded to ask a question about my research. Fumbling initially, I recovered and delivered a formal response. We chatted a bit longer and I then completed my formal presentation. As I was making my way out she said, "Good luck, you have a very nice voice."

I'll never forget this person sitting down in the late evening and listening to what I had to say, then making the genuine effort to be involved and help me.

One way to signal respect for people is to involve them more: you may elect to include junior people in some decision-making. This makes them feel respected and challenged by the need to think outside their traditional responsibilities. It's a unique opportunity for them to participate; your respect will be rewarded with loyalty.

Fairness

Treat people fairly: fair compensation and equal opportunity.

Fair Compensation: People can, and do, benchmark their compensation to market norms: you have to pay at least the representative market rates to attract and/or retain qualified staff.

If you insist on lower compensation, it is a given that your employees will realize that you offer/pay below-norm salaries: unless you are able to complement the below-standard salaries with desirable non-pecuniary compensation such as shorter hours, telecommuting, or unusual benefits, you will face expensive, time-consuming staff turnover when you can least afford the time and energy to recruit and hire replacement staff.

A scenario typical for ailing firms: management is under pressure to control costs; their response is clamping down on salaries and bonuses, setting off a vicious cycle. Employees resent the lower salaries; some decide to leave. Managers subsequently spend time and resources replacing them; resources spent replacing personnel are taken away from efforts to remedy the firm's underlying problems; the firm cannot make progress; the cash crunch continues, leading to more cost-cutting measures which lower morale even further and cause more departures, including people who recently joined.

It doesn't take too long before word gets out that the firm pays poorly: it becomes even more difficult to attract good people.

Instead of allowing this to happen to you and your firm, you can break the cycle by selectively penalizing only those employees who deserve it: those who perform poorly. The money saved by withholding undeserved raises and bonuses along with other cost-cutting can be redirected to retaining your best performers. The challenge in this process is to properly distinguish the good employees from the poor performers via employee performance evaluations.

A fair compensation scheme will keep the good employees on board; the poor performers have a choice: leave, or elect to modify their behavior, contribute more and perform better for the firm. Your role is creating a fair performance evaluation system, and compensating based on that system. How people react is up to them. Note that a fair system, by its design, may encourage departure of the poor performers.

Equal Opportunity: Few factors demoralize people more than realizing that their success and progress is unfairly restricted. Identify such situations and reverse them.

The first priority is to address deeply embedded systemic practices: hiring only "people like us," compensation scales based on race, gender, ethnicity or other illegal standards. Changing such practices requires confronting the inequities at the highest levels of policy makers, considerable time, patience and effort, and perhaps a few dismissals "for cause" of senior management and/or human resources staff responsible for violating the spirit and letter of the law.

Strive for fair opportunities, advancement, recognition, and rewards; spreading opportunities around equitably means more people will have a chance to succeed and to be recognized. This balance will ensure that no individual or group feels consistently disadvantaged. Furthermore, by giving credit where it's due, you will ensure that credit isn't borrowed by the undeserving.

The challenge, of course, is that the distressed firm may not have sufficient resources to reward everyone simultaneously: it may not be possible to provide desired opportunities to all who request them; it may not be possible to promote all the deserving candidates, simply because more senior roles may not exist.

Establish a straightforward, transparent system so people know, with reasonable certainty, where they stand. You must choose the standards for promotion carefully: seniority, such as years of service to the firm, may be a measure of political savvy, rather than effective contribution; seniority is a legitimate measure to determine who receives the next promotion opportunity *so long as it's combined with required skills and a good performance record.* Otherwise, the firm is not a meritocracy.

Your personal discipline and sense of fairness is especially important: if you don't like someone personally, you may have a natural inclination to rule against the person when disagreements arise. You cannot allow yourself to be unfair.

Rule each case on its own merits, exercising every bit of emotional intelligence, intuition, and objectivity you possess.

Suspend your prejudices, biases, and personal preferences unrelated to employee performance (you don't like short people, or people taller than you, or people with hard-to-pronounce names).

Quality

It's important that you set the bar for performance as high as possible, while still attainable. Undertake tasks in an orderly fashion, and do each well. Encourage all employees to do the same. A poorly done job is not really "done" at all. Worse than that, it's wasteful.

Make it clear to people that if they do something improperly, they create a weak link in business processes, and eventually someone else will have to go back and mend the damage.

Besides being inefficient, the need to revisit always seems to happen at the worst possible moment: the software solution you sold to a client breaks down just after your best technology expert has left for a two-week vacation—in a remote place with no phone service—where he is completely incommunicado.

A troubled firm already has more than its fair share of weak links and trouble spots; employees must understand that removing the weaknesses and replacing them with high quality, reliable processes is a part of everyone's job. Managers unfamiliar with the requirements for complying with certain regulatory rules, for example, might not recognize a flawed process: the more junior person who has to do the job probably will. Everyone's input is needed.

Example: If you are reading an employee's work for the first time, look at it carefully; take the opportunity to observe and provide constructive feedback, emphasizing excellence. Are the statements accurate? Is it professionally written? Is there an acceptable level of language skills? Are there any glaring, or subtle, errors? Take advantage of the opportunity to evaluate performance and educate. When you do this thoughtfully, you encourage others to do the same: this lesson is very important for new managers, who are used to looking at their own work, but are not familiar with the need to examine the work of others and provide meaningful, educational, constructive feedback.

Learn which of your employees are competitive and respond positively to challenges, and which ones find pressure to compete internally disrespectful and debasing. The latter are often the folks who already *know* their abilities and their worth, who find endless goal-setting, contests, and "carrots" distracting and undignified. Pay them what they're worth, and let them get on with their jobs. In contrast, seek ways to challenge those in the former group.

Some people are competitive by nature; collaborate with them and set mutual, reachable goals that push them, but not beyond the breaking point. You and/or direct managers of competitors must be actively involved to ensure that ambition is tempered with pragmatism, and that goals are finely tuned to push people toward excellence at a manageable, constructive pace.

Enthusiasm

To set the tone for everyone else, be enthusiastic.

You must hold the soul of your company in your heart.

Enthusiasm is the soul of positive momentum; engaging others with your genuine enthusiasm for the Mission, spreading your positive sense of accomplishments-to-come is infectious.

Set the right, enthusiastic tone; walk into the office every day with a genuine smile and say "Good Morning!" to everyone you meet. Whenever you are walking the floor, be mindful of your effect on others: no striding forcefully, head down, hands fisted; no frowning.

Engage in small talk, connect with people. Hearing genuine, positive praise from the boss is inspiring to everyone; *absolutely no sarcasm, "damning with faint praise," or otherwise-hypocritical behavior is allowable from you or any other manager.*

Never underestimate the power of a genuine smile: smiles can put people at ease, defuse difficult situations, and bridge cultural divides when verbal communication is insufficient; smiles are contagious. Kick off the trend in the executive suite.

Make sure your assistant has a sunny disposition and a ready smile. This is a talent (and you should pay well for it) affecting colleagues, clients, and everyone else who comes to visit you. It also helps you to stay positive.

Do you like going to the office and being greeted by grumpy, prickly, discourteous people? The answer is obvious: far too many people fail to fully consider their public disposition.

You can probably name at least one person in your workplace who consistently displays unpleasant and depressing characteristics. Everyone has "down" days; the concern is with the adverse effects one (or a few) individuals' negative, depressing behavior patterns wreak. Their presence can become a negative refrain, every bit as aggravating as a song you don't particularly like, running endlessly through your mind..

Malcontents slow the firm's momentum; their anxiety-producing distractions pull people away from value creation.

If a person exhibiting this behavior is a manager, his negative energy will be directed at all his direct reports, causing much greater destruction of momentum and value, not to mention the emotional toll on staff.

Imagine the systemic damage a leader can inflict with such destructive behavior!

Negativity is widespread in distressed firms, often reaching the top: when dissatisfaction, discontent, and disappointment *emanates* from the top, firms die. Sometimes the demise is quick and painful; more often, it is *slow* and painful demise.

Complaining and other offensive behavior chases away talent, wastes time, deflates enthusiasm, and generally serves no purpose other than shooting everyone in the foot. Joking aside, managers who frustrate staff occasionally find themselves at the wrong end of real bullets fired by disgruntled employees.

Everyone has "off" days; but the leader simply cannot afford to shout angrily at people, throw things, knock things off his desk, kick the waste basket, or otherwise lose his self-control.

Show that you are unsettled and you will unsettle everyone else; remain tranquil in the face of bad news and setbacks, and you send an important message of calm and control.

When you are discouraged, fatigued, or vulnerable to losing your self-control, take a break! Take a walk, meditate, listen to your favorite music for 15 minutes; call someone you love just to hear their voice, daydream, read the jokes in your e-mail. Breathe deeply. When was the last time you ate? Take care of yourself.

Communication

"Business Communications" is a subject so complex it has become a degree program in top business schools around the globe. Appreciating the difficulty and significance of both interpersonal and organizational communications does not require a degree in the subject.

All communication influences people, for good or ill; within a company whose viability is in question, where people fear loss of bonus, loss of job, loss of face, their emotional states make them particularly vulnerable to misunderstanding and misinterpretation.

Weigh your words carefully, knowing they have the power to uplift or destroy; be certain your facial expressions are consistent with your message. If you are saying reassuring words while frowning, listeners who can see you are distracted by the discord between words and expression. This doesn't mean changing your message: express your thoughts carefully, precisely; praise honestly; criticize constructively and in timely fashion. Rehearse your facial expressions in a mirror if you have previously observed that people are puzzled or unsure of your meaning. Watch how others react to you, privately, one-on-one, as well as publicly in a formal group, informal settings, and casual gatherings.

Example: Early in my career I attended my private company's annual "town hall" meeting for a discussion of employee compensation. A colleague asked our CEO about the way the firm's value was being calculated, and, after receiving an answer, voiced concerns about unfair implications for stock-option grants.

The CEO, frustrated that the conversation wasn't progressing as planned, dismissively stated that the employee's opinion didn't matter, and pressed on. It was clear to all present that the CEO didn't want to communicate openly on this subject; there was broad sympathy for the employee who had asked a legitimate question and instead of an answer suffered an insult.

The outcome was that trust in the CEO decreased markedly. The employee, irreparably offended, lost faith in management and left the firm shortly after.

Make sure discussions among staff members are constructive. It's too easy (and common) for comments and feedback among colleagues to be interpreted as personally-motivated antagonism. Help steer people to making constructive comments, and to accepting them as such.

Once there is a perceived offense, it's easy to fall into a cycle of retaliation and mutual recrimination. Both sides feel victimized, and both are much less inclined to cooperate in future.

Allow people to voice concerns and objections to decisions made by you and others; first, be certain that the individual(s) fully understand(s) the decision; is it a real disagreement, or is there a disconnect between the individual's knowledge and your explanation of the decision? If the disagreement is based in a legitimate question, you have to answer the question fully and directly, and persuade him to cooperate.

You may find yourself frustrated by questions and disagreements, and want to say, "Just do as I say!" Quell that impulse: disagreeing with you does not make him an extremist. Totalitarian rulers label those who dissent "extremists" and remove them. Modern firms cannot succeed under totalitarian rule. The leader's job is to discern the difference between a simple disagreement, when an employee just voices an opinion, and an employee crossing the line from constructive comment and debate to poisoning the work environment.

Every member of the team is obligated to think critically and participate in problem-solving discussions. There is value in dissent and constructive opposing views; avoiding unintended consequences is chief among them. Extremists are inflexible, espouse opinions vehemently, are often verbally aggressive or attempt intellectual intimidation through sarcasm or "damn with faint praise." Their motto is, "Don't confuse me with facts, my mind is made up!"

It's legitimate and necessary to remove such people from interaction with colleagues, not only to protect morale, but to establish your authority.

Truly uncooperative and inflexible people will have demonstrated such behavior in past encounters; be sure your human resources group has a plan in place for disciplining employees, including a series of steps beginning with corrective actions and culminating with dismissal "for cause" in extreme cases.

Frustration preceding your arrival may lead reasonable people to appear uncooperative early on; those who have been under stress for a long time need to express their legitimate concerns; the only way you will know those concerns is to invite their comments and opinions. Don't judge people until you have given them a chance to settle down.

When you are about to address any group, whether in person, by phone, through a web cast, as a panelist or speaker, always find out who will attend and what their interests or concerns may be. Will these people have an axe to grind? Is the session expected to be confrontational or friendly? Strained or relaxed? If it is an external presentation, should you anticipate the competition's presence? Is there any likelihood you will be "ambushed" at this event? Will the event be videotaped, audio taped, transcribed?

Prepare as carefully for key internal presentations as you would for external ones. Staff, especially early on, will be looking to you for direction, inspiration, and answers. Not having a credible response will be perceived negatively. Practice the content, delivery, and tone of your speech, and try to anticipate tough or sensitive questions.

Decide who, inside and outside the firm, will make external presentations and speak to the media; announce to junior staff—particularly those who answer telephones!—to whom *all* media inquiries should be routed. Teach them how to graciously redirect aggressive inquirers to your designated speakers. Make sure you, and all other designated speakers, receive media training to avoid mishaps, *faux pas*, and statements too open to (mis)interpretations. Establish with management, the Board, parent company, partners, etc., where the lines separate *"do's"* and *"don'ts."* What can you say, what can you not say, about corporate initiatives, policies, financial reports, public investigations, etc.?

Ensure Your Message is Received and Understood

Merely delivering a message does not qualify as "successful communication." Your intended message must reach your intended audience; it must be *understood* by that audience.

Using paper or e-mail reports to communicate is not necessarily effective because the report may never be read. Even when it is read, if written without brevity, clarity, eloquence and passion, the message may be lost.

Follow text communiqués with human contact: at least a phone call to ensure the message was received and understood. Any hint that the message has not been received or understood requires prompt, explicit follow-up—if a face-to-face meeting isn't practical, schedule a video conference or an appointment for a telephone conversation. Sending an agenda for the discussion, along with any appropriate documents, is a professional courtesy; it helps you clarify your ideas, and others can prepare themselves fully. *Never waste anyone's time, especially yours.*

Communicating effectively with stakeholders, such as senior management and the Board, is central to every business, particularly in a turnaround environment. The last thing you need is for your management to misunderstand the key messages you are striving to deliver; you have to ensure the message is delivered *and* heard.

Whether or not they accept your ideas and recommendations is up to them: stakeholders' failure to comprehend an important message (even if you sent it) will be held against *you*. Conclusion: keep the stakeholders informed. No one likes surprises; negative surprises that embarrass stakeholders will cause confusion, mistrust, and, perhaps, unfortunate public statements.

Example: *I recently witnessed a CEO who was asked by his direct report for permission to proceed with a certain action. The answer was yes and the junior executive pressed on. Several days later, upon hearing of the junior executive's actions, the chief executive summoned him and criticized him for moving forward.*

Here is the exchange that followed, beginning with the junior's confusion:

- *"But you said 'yes' when I asked about this?"*

- *"I know I said 'yes,' but there are different types of 'yes'."*

- *"How am I supposed to know when 'yes' means 'no'?"*

- *"You should be able to tell from the way I say it."*

This is an interesting example, because it can be interpreted in at least two ways:

On the one hand, one may argue that the junior's emotional intelligence should lead him to read the manager's nuanced intention.

On the other hand, a manager who expects staff members to figure out which "yes" he means is setting the stage for confusion and inconsistency.

The most responsible interpretation is that, in this instance, the CEO was at fault. He broke the cardinal rule of effective communication: *"Say what you mean so you cannot be misunderstood."*

Nuanced interpretation is too much to expect, particularly from younger, less experienced people. The CEOs behavior subsequently led to uncertainty for all employees who heard the story, leading to great inefficiencies as all junior managers repeatedly second-guessed their own understanding of instructions, wondering whether their interpretation might lead to ridicule or punishment.

A CEO who expects staff to read his mind, or deliberately makes "deniable" statements is *creating* additional dysfunction—the last thing a troubled firm needs.

More than ever before, our business reality is characterized by multi-culturalism and remote communication: everyone has to deal with confusing accents, cultural differences in communication styles, and reduced personal contact due to proliferation of e-mail and conference calls. Under these conditions, expecting others (at any level) to pick up on nuances and body language is asking for trouble. Be direct and be clear. Say what you mean so you cannot be misunderstood.

If you find that the stakeholders refuse to accept the message, or consistently refuse to open the channels of communication (refuse to meet you for clarification), and subsequently "shoot the messenger," you are stuck in an unhealthy situation.

You must have the full support of your seniors to be effective; anything less puts you on shaky ground. You can not build anything, or turn around any enterprise, with a shaky foundation. If important people refuse to allow you to communicate effectively, and you do not have the means of overcoming their influence, it may be time to look elsewhere.

Abolish Wasteful Meetings

Meetings are the cornerstone of human communication, the preferred forum for solving and resolving, sharing thoughts and emotions, building trust, collaborating, reaching consensus, and making decisions.

When utilized effectively, meetings are an efficient and useful vehicle to disseminate information, educate people, and obtain their feedback. When not utilized properly, meetings can multiply inefficiencies and waste. How can meetings be so wasteful?

Let us count the ways:

1. Each attendee, who would, presumably, be productive doing something other than attending the meeting in question, represents an opportunity cost.

2. The logistical expenditures for getting everyone together—travel costs, lodging, meals, videoconference facilities, extra phone lines—in addition to the time wasted in airports, finding a shuttle or taxi, can far exceed the value of the decisions reached at the meeting.

3. One attendee can create a tremendous amount of waste and drag down the productivity of many colleagues. Every minute a person is late; every minute a person spends on tangential issues during discussion; every minute of disruptive arguments, is multiplied by the number of attendees. This is "meeting math."

   10 people are present: 1 person hijacks the conversation for 15 minutes, he has wasted 10x15 = 150 minutes = 2.5 hours of the company's time! If the *average* earnings of those 10

people is $50,000 per year, the digressions will cost about $600.

If this person repeatedly causes distractions over the course of an entire day, the waste can easily amount to 8 or 10 hours—the productivity of an entire person for a full day, all wasted.

If the waste always comes from one source there is a simple answer: don't allow the person in question into meetings, or try to convince him to join the competition.

4. Typically, multiple people introduce inefficiencies; few people don't, at least once in a while, contribute to tangential conversations and distractions. Thus, one way to wring out inefficiencies is to focus on the meeting culture of an organization and streamline it.

As a first step, you must show others how to conduct an efficient meeting:

- Write the agenda: define the issues to be addressed;

- Allocate reasonable time to cover the agenda fully—no more, no less.

- Invite only those people who will benefit from, and provide benefit to, the discussion.

- Start on time.

- End on time.

- Have someone take notes; circulate these to attendees. Designate someone (other than chief participants) who is smart enough to keep up, confident enough to ask for clarification when needed to ensure accuracy, and can be trusted not to mis-quote or mis-attribute statements.

- Keep everyone on point; intervene if the conversation wanders.

- Call people to order if their behavior warrants rebuke. Setting the example early will make it very clear to all concerned that unconstructive behavior won't be tolerated.

- Do not interrupt the flow of discussion to bring late arrivals up to speed.

  A. It's tempting to think that slowing down for them is the right thing to do, even the polite thing to do. Unless their tardiness is completely unavoidable, it is the *late-comers* who are being disrespectful.

  B, The other (respectful) attendees sit idly by while this impromptu update takes place, wasting discussion momentum and person-hours.

  C. Allowing participants to be admitted late to meetings is a disservice to those who have made an effort to be prompt, and gives the "prompt" good reason to lose faith in the usefulness of the meeting, and skip meetings in future.

  D. Set up a separate update session for those who are unavoidably delayed by cancelled flights, traffic accidents or other delays *outside their control.*

- When attendees are habitually tardy and or make "the dog ate my briefcase" excuses, simply tell them they can read the minutes or notes of the meeting.

In addition to the considerations listed above, keep in mind that meetings are an opportunity for you to learn about your staff:

- Ensure the environment is conducive to achieving your objective. Should you sit at your large desk, on your fancy, high chair, facing the visitors on their smaller, intimidated perches? Or do you have a round table you and your colleagues can sit around as equals? What message are you sending with each approach?

- Observe people's social behavior. How well do they handle themselves? Do they exhibit understanding, open-mindedness, empathy for the positions and concerns of others? Do they interact constructively, use the occasion for personal attacks?

- Make note of people's strengths and weaknesses. Follow up with individuals, or with their direct managers, to ensure feedback is provided to them, praising and critiquing as relevant.

Some people infer they are obligated to speak a lot to justify their presence, especially when a senior person, who implies a desire to be impressed, attends. Any manager who leads others into such behavior is probably in need of an attitude adjustment, particularly when long, wasteful meetings result.

As the manager/moderator, set the tone early by refocusing the discussions; do not allow people to engage in irrelevant speech-making, repeating what has already been said, or arguing for the sake of arguing. Each meeting, however impromptu, must have an objective; every participant must strive toward realizing that goal.

Example: Here is an example of management contributing to the "delinquency of participants" by creating such an intimidating environment that people often failed to present themselves and their opinions successfully.

I was in the Board room of a Fortune 500 company to provide an update on my unit's performance. The meeting began with junior executives filing in, shaking hands. Then more-senior people entered, and joined the ritual. This was followed by even more-senior executives entering and shaking hands, and so on until the CEO arrived. He purposely timed his entry to be the last person, to ensure that all eyes were on him. He then took his seat at the head of the table.

As we realized the enormous room would not be full, we rookies moved to the table and lined up behind some chairs within speaking distance of the CEO. As we moved to these chairs, one of the senior executives stopped us with a gesture, and used another quick gesture to direct us to the other end of the table. We padded over and sat at the end. One of us prepared to sit at the very end of the table, which would have put him directly opposite the CEO. Yet another senior executive's gesture disabused him of this precocious notion and he moved off to the side.

The executives then went through their almost comical seating ritual, arranging themselves by seniority, with the most-senior flanking the CEO, and the less- and less-senior ones radiating out from there on both sides.

It soon became clear that the same segregationist culture applied when it was time to "discuss." Stern glances quickly and silently delivered the message that one didn't speak unless spoken to, or asked a question by one of the senior executives.

This wooden ritual consumed 90 minutes, and then it was time to rise and file out. No handshaking, no mingling, just an ushering out of the "little" people.

No doubt, the senior executives who'd spent decades fighting for access to the C-suite felt this was an important tradition; they had earned their place at the table.

There is also little doubt that many of those subjected to these rituals came away with significantly reduced respect for the senior management of the company. How could they possibly waste their time on such inanity, when all that energy could be directed more productively? How could they possibly expect to know what was going on throughout the company when they never spent any time on any floor other than the executive floor at the top of the building?

Returning now to the topic of *productive* meetings, it's important to consider why many people are reluctant to participate. Some reasons may include:

- They see meetings as a big waste of time. Perhaps they have never attended a properly conducted meeting.

- They are not prepared, and want to avoid the embarrassment of having the fact revealed to their peers, managers, and direct reports.

- They are afraid of speaking in a public setting.

The remedies for these issues are quite simple:

- Take to heart the above discussion of how efficient meetings should be conducted: hold meetings only when you have a specific purpose, and the meeting adds value. Take the time to explain why these sessions are important.

- Create an environment that brings people together constructively, comfortably, and non-judgmentally. Expect participants to be thoroughly prepared.

- Encourage people to participate fully. When necessary, work with their mentors to gradually bring them out of their shells. Praise and mentor them to defuse any lingering traumas.

You want and need people to contribute everything they can; it's a direct loss to the firm if someone has a good idea or comment, but is too shy or bored to contribute. Do not let this happen: build forums for information exchange into schedules; use them to accomplish tangible objectives, including learning about, and educating, staff.

Calling people to order if their behavior crosses the line into destructive behavior is necessary. One of your critical roles is to decide where that line is. Sometimes this is obvious. Using foul language or intimidating behavior leads to tension and anxiety; either warrants quick intervention.

In contrast, *creative* tension contributes to a constructive learning environment; when you or your employees face other colleagues and hear their passionate arguments, the intensity can convey details and concerns that a measured monotone cannot.

Creative tension in supportive environments can lead all participants to better understanding of others' work, greater appreciation of their challenges and frustrations, and open processes to new ideas, collaboration, and real problem-solving.

Those who exhibit intensity and passion may benefit from the opportunity to truly explain their perspectives. It is always your responsibility to decide whether the intensity is, or is not, serving a positive purpose. Passion can fuel positive momentum or destroy it, depending upon whether the passion is properly harnessed and directed.

At all times, praise in public, and criticize in private. That is, congratulate people for a job well done in front of their peers, allowing them to bask in the glow of a compliment, while providing a model for the others to follow. In contrast, to avoid embarrassment, use private moments to indicate to people where and how they may have made mistakes or crossed lines into inappropriate behavior. This is particularly important to individuals who lack emotional intelligence and or emotional competence: they simply do not understand how they look to others, why their behavior impacts others, and how to intuit the social rules of a given group.

Leadership by Example

Managers can always direct people to do things, but setting a personal example is the most sustainable way to inspire people to *voluntarily* follow your direction. At all times, what you say and what you do must be consistent: the smallest hint of hypocrisy will turn the very people you need most against you.

Leading by example is requisite in every managerial setting: some managers believe they can "act" the part, not understanding the difference between being politically astute (acceptable), and political machination (unacceptable).

Example: *I once had a boss who took great pride in his political exploits within our large firm. He had an extensive network of connections, and a great amount of influence, most of it due to having ridden the coattails of a very senior Executive Vice President, to whom he showed unwavering loyalty.*

Whenever I indicated to him that I was uncomfortable with a particular path because it seemed too politically self-serving, he would give me a lecture about the meaning of the word politics (from the Greek "polis", effectively referring to "things concerning state or city affairs"). He would proudly emphasize that engaging in politics is at the heart of being a manager.

Undoubtedly, awareness of how best to deal with people for their own good and that of their organization (or city, or state) is a required skill for a leader. Over time, however, I came to realize that his speeches covered up the fact that his politicking had nothing to do with assisting people and their organizations in reaching their full potential. Rather, it was designed to maintain his position of influence, often by blindly agreeing to decisions made by his benefactor, the Executive Vice President. He never disagreed with this mentor, and never subjected the latter's decisions to his own conscience.

Ultimate responsibility for a firm's troubles rests with its management; when a firm is a turnaround candidate, the previous management were doing some things wrong. The new management team, under your direction, has to begin the reformation process. The proper, credible way to do this is by leading from the front.

Your poise, attitude, and demeanor set a standard; the tasks you take on personally and the manner in which you pursue them effectively demonstrate that "this is really important and I want to personally make sure it's executed properly."

Strive to identify those areas in which the standard was not properly set by the previous management, and communicate your new approach clearly and consistently. It's important that disgruntled employees are able to distinguish the differences between the former, failed approach, and your new, effective approach. They need to observe your personal commitment to doing what's necessary to reach a successful conclusion.

To keep up with you, your immediate circle will have to commit to your priorities and techniques. In turn, their direct reports must focus on the same issues. This cascade will continue until your preferences have permeated the entire organization.

Some examples of how you can constructively set the tone:

- If you want to have a commitment to research and development, put yourself on the R&D task force that examines all new product ideas. Require that all research be pursued with rigor and persistence; model the attitudes and behaviors you expect. If you can, take charge of initial meetings yourself; set the agendas, clarify the mission, set priorities. If chairing the task force is too logistically challenging, assign conducting the meetings to others; however, be actively involved in discussions and decisions. Follow up with people who contributed and make it known that you have done so.

- If you want to establish a commitment to client service, spend time with both the decision-makers and staff assigned to day-to-day service for existing clients. Take other executives with you to client meetings, include the relevant relationship managers; ensure that your commitment is visible to your entire company. Inject the direct feedback from clients into internal reports and conversations—formal and informal. Follow-up on the outcomes; make it clear to your staff that you take client concerns seriously, and expect them to do the same. If spending long hours with clients requires travel or a host location, budget for the expense.

- If you want to establish a commitment to sales, go on as many sales calls as you can. Take the account managers and regional managers with you, and follow up with them after the calls to check on progress. Your involvement throughout the sales cycle will also allow you to identify any weaknesses in your sales staff or their processes. You will subsequently be in a position to make appropriate recommendations to address any such weaknesses.

The need for follow-up has been emphasized in each of the examples above. The follow-up is critical: it establishes that you care about more than just the initial meeting; you care about *success*. A squeaky wheel gets attention, but only until another wheel begins to squeak: an urgent need may be addressed, but when attention is distracted by the next crisis (in a troubled firm there's always a "next crisis" looming), your squeaky wheel may come loose, and fail completely.

When people observe you taking an active, ongoing interest long after the squeaks are fixed, and continue until the job is done, you are modeling commitment, showing that you expect them to take notice and act in concert.

Some people's renewed commitment and action will result from genuine affinity for your leadership: others will do so for less-respectable reasons. They will act simply because you're the boss. They may not care that your way is better than others. Regardless of the motivation, at least you've got people acting in concert, with their energies focused in the direction you have set. Over time, you may actually convert the nonbelievers, but hypocrites who simply pretend to support you probably never will change their own private agendas.

Turnaround firms are often financially strapped: the need to cut costs may be desperate. Share the pain of the cost-cutting, up to and including restructuring your base salary, and/or accepting a much smaller (or zero) bonus.

Leadership by example can be very hard when it is so difficult to discern the wisest response to the multitude of problems you face; be clear with everyone that you are focused on the company's survival.

Intense and focused fact-gathering reflects your intellectual clarity and experience. Treating people respectfully, being scrupulously honest, displaying unflinching integrity and fairness, setting high behavior standards and demanding excellence make you accountability personified, founder of the new culture of confidence and enthusiasm for the future.

Decisiveness

Dysfunctional firms *always* suffer from leaders who lack decisiveness. One may argue which is the cause and which the effect, but once both indecision and dysfunction are present, they are mutually reinforcing. The only way to break this damaging cycle is for you, the leader, to make decisions quickly.

The early period of your appointment is critical: it sets the tone for your tenure. Identify the causes of the firm's problems and take action to reverse or remedy them as soon as possible. Quick decision-making and action are also critical to sending the message to all staff, clients, and suppliers that the bad times are coming to an end because someone capable is in charge.

Of course, the big challenge is that because you are new, you may not know enough to make decisions early on.

No one said leadership is easy.

Example: *I recall sitting in my first senior management meeting. I had recently been promoted to lead the firm's product strategy efforts, and although I was a junior Director, this position gave me "a seat at the table" with the senior managing directors.*

The new President casually convened the meeting, welcomed me with a wide smile, and everyone responded with their own beaming smiles. I felt immediately comfortable and looked forward to all the achievements this power group would be able to institute.

The President completed his opening remarks outlining the agenda for the day, which would begin with a discussion of the state of the market and demand for our products. He then turned the floor over to the Global Head of Sales. The Global Head of Sales began his response with the phrase, "I may be speaking out of ignorance but I think…" Based on what he said, I couldn't help silently observing that he really did appear to be speaking out of ignorance. Next, the floor was turned over to the Global Head of Research. To my astonishment, he also began his comments with "I'm probably also somewhat ignorant of the latest market forces, but …" I was subsequently only slightly surprised, when the Head of Global Product Management began his commentary with a similar disclaimer, and quickly redirected the question to me, in my capacity as "the new Head of Product Strategy." I passionately fired off several sentences summarizing my thoughts about prevailing market forces and implications for us and then, being young and naïve (and very foolish), I added, "and I'm not speaking out of ignorance. This is what's happening out there."

I can still picture a roomful of MDs struggling not to fall off their chairs, and the President turning to look me in the eye with a look combining both surprise and amusement.

This reflects a common Boardroom problem. The new CEO was surrounded by people who were unwilling to take a firm stand, either because they were afraid to stand out, or because they really were ignorant. An entire work force of three hundred people were struggling in the trenches, while in the Boardroom, everyone was "ignorant." Why were they running the firm if they are so ignorant? Imagine what the President thought every time this useless group convened to make plans. Imagine his frustration at trying to turn around a struggling firm with so little contribution from his immediate circle. Most important, how could he make any real decisions?

Take heart: you don't have to make perfect decisions Day One. Don't burden yourself at all with the notion your decisions have to be perfect. *No one* makes *perfect* decisions. It's generally a good start to just make a few solid decisions relatively quickly. Military (and corporate) leaders will tell you it's better to make a decent decision quickly than to wait endlessly for the perfect plan to materialize. By the time you get to that perfect plan, the enemy or competitor will have overrun your position and your markets.

Your level of empowerment is highest when you are new on the job. The authority vested in you by an enthusiastic management or Board is at its peak when you first join, while you are still basking in the aura of (untested) perfection and they are relieved they have finally found a solution to their leadership problem. Thereafter, you have a brief honeymoon, and the next thing you know, your (formerly) biggest fans are asking, politely at first, "What have you done for me lately?"

A troubled firm is like quicksand: if you are not proactive, you will eventually be sucked into business-as-usual, and it will become ever harder to break out of an increasingly lethargic state.

Your Maxim #1: Make changes early. If you fail to impact the organization positively early on, your future effectiveness will be limited.

Your Maxim #2: The longer you wait, the weaker you become.

It's relatively easy to take over a smoothly running, successful business, staffed by good people. Yes, you can mismanage, but as a capable leader you should make enough correct choices not to throw a bearing in a well-oiled machine. Dysfunctional settings afford you none of the luxuries found in successful organizations. A much higher percentage of your decisions are crucial: the downside is making a mistake will loom larger.

All human organizations have common characteristics: corporations have to be structured according to laws; businesses within industries have similarities, and all are subject to macroeconomic and market forces.

Choose the business functions most vulnerable to dysfunction to review first; some specific dysfunctions will be obvious, others more subtle. All dysfunctions will be revealed in time; identify enough of them within your first few weeks to figure out how to make meaningful contributions; act decisively; set the stage for change. Nothing else will help morale more than decisive, ethical leadership.

Identify points of conflict; resolve these as soon as possible. Organizations formed by mergers and acquisitions are likely to spawn conflicts over levels of executive and management authority, and may even have units with conflicting missions.

Example: *Global firms created by merger and acquisition may suffer from discord because of traditional differences in management structures and compensation schemes. A European CEO may find he is paid considerably less than an American counterpart, and so on down the executive line. Negotiating and selling equitable compensation schemes requires great finesse and diplomacy.*

Stop the departure of talented people; you may have to rely on sheer charisma to capture their hearts and minds and inspire them to stay. Your emotional intelligence and competence are essential to ensuring these people remain engaged and committed.

Do not be held hostage to fear that people will leave if you make decisions they dislike; if people threaten to leave unless treated preferentially, *help* them leave.

Welcome healthy debate—after all, you are new; listen to others' opinions, make the best decisions possible and carry them out. Individual team members must learn to accept some outcomes that do not match their personal preferences—including your most senior personnel.

Encourage staff to wring inefficiencies out of their decision-making processes:

- One useful exercise is to have staff estimate the amount of time it takes each of them to respond to a particular request: reviewing, commenting, requesting clarification, and ultimately approving a course of action.

- Multiply their time by individuals' hourly or annual wages; add together all the hours/dollars to calculate the cost of *making* that particular decision.

- The cost of *making* the decision is *in addition* to the funds for the expenditure.

Knowing these costs provides a much better understanding of how (in)efficient decision-making hierarchies are within the firm. Consider the earlier example of the employee attempting to collect her travel expense reimbursement: when a simple, procedural decision takes so much *executive* time, one wonders how much profit is lost in such outrageous overhead costs.

An important element of decisiveness is the courage to act boldly. The most effective strategy may simply be to change the ground rules:

- Create new policy that encourages boldness. Seek out those who made an effort, but their project fell short: commend them publicly for their courage.

- Work with them to understand why the outcome was unfavorable; share the findings with others, admire the efforts and consolidate the learning in the company's culture.

- Recognize every setback as learning and coaching opportunities: the most shocking failures and dismal disasters are memorable, on-the-job learning experiences. Objectively and fairly analyzed, hindsight yields true insights the individual is unlikely to forget.

CHAPTER 7
Plan the Turnaround

Create Plans for Tackling the Turnaround

In turnaround situations, existing plans are usually flawed or non-existent. Asking for copies of the current "plans" before you accept the position is an excellent way to gauge how knowledgeable the people recruiting you really are about the depths of dysfunction they're asking you to fix. Some immediate thoughts regarding plans:

- If you have no Mission Statement, you have no clear, concise "gold standard" for staff to follow in making their own judgment calls.

- If you have no Value Propositions, you are limiting your own company's sales: if you cannot explain to the customer why your widget is better than Brand X, and show how it will improve you customer's business, you have no sale.

- The Business Plan is among the first documents lenders and investors ask to see: if you don't have one, you have no tool for attracting funds.

The process of formulating Mission Statements, Value Propositions and Business Plans is your first, best opportunity to reinvent this company according to your best judgment, imprint your vision upon your staff, and empower them.

Detailed and defensible Mission Statements, Value Propositions and Business Plans are the blueprints for the firm's emergence from distress: formulating them is urgent because they constitute your Corporate Canon: your reference for decision-making. Every short-, mid-, and long-term decision has to be consistent with all three documents.

Scientists who speak of "elegant" solutions mean their answer is "gracefully concise and simple, admirably succinct." Strive for elegance in your Mission Statements, Business Plans, and Value Propositions. Admirably succinct phrases are simple to remember when a decision must be made under pressure.

Mission Statement: The Mission Statement is the collective vision of the firm's _raison d'etre_ ("reason for being"), stated as simply, concisely and eloquently as possible.

If this Mission Statement is not uniformly embraced, it's meaningless: select staff with the skills, integrity and inclination to match the Mission Statement and its underlying values.

If your Mission is excellent client service, seek people with outstanding client service abilities. Build the Mission into company culture: tie performance goals and incentive pay to excellent customer service.

If your Mission is to develop ground-breaking new technologies, pursue outstanding researchers, provide them with the tools and environment necessary: prize and reward ideation and prototyping.

Value Proposition: A Value Proposition (VP) is usually product and market segment-specific; write it in compelling, positive language to set your company apart, emphasize what your firm can do for the client, and differentiate your solutions from the competitors'.

When you first look at a well-written Value Proposition, you may think "Well, duh!" because it seems so simple, so obvious, so elegant. Profound, compelling statements are among the most difficult to articulate; forming the right Value Proposition is no exception. It calls for deep, insightful, and forward-looking understanding of a client's needs (often before the client realizes their need), then offering a solution that solves real problems, saves the client money, makes the client money, or all three.

An "all purpose" Value Proposition will not be compelling unless you have *one* product, *one* service, or *one* client. The process of imagining how to diversify your offerings and customer base is an excellent "brainstorming" technique to lead you to new markets, identify prospects, study their needs, and sell your wares.

Consider the following questions:

- How should client segments be defined?

- How many distinct segments are there?

- Is it cost-efficient to target many, or only a few, segments?

- Given the importance of focus and impact, which client segments are most critical and deserve your earliest attention?

You must understand the characteristics of each client segment to answer these questions.

Understanding client characteristics requires documenting, through meaningful client contact, the key elements of each solution that helps them do their job better. You must involve your client service, sales, product engineers, product managers, and marketing staff in the process.

This process, correctly done, imposes much-needed discipline, and forces teams to set aside old assumptions and answer hard questions. You may realize certain existing products have to be altered, delivered differently, or terminated. Building sustainable momentum requires this clarity and pragmatism, and may require additional staff development.

Example: *Prepare your staff members for client meetings and debrief them after the fact. Those in traditionally non-client facing roles, such as engineers and operations personnel, will likely need some coaching.*

Prior to the meeting, explain to them what they are likely to encounter. Point out that an objective of the meeting is to understand the client's needs, and the individual viewpoints of client's staff. Some may be supportive of your firm; others may be opponents. Identifying these motives requires examination of body language, innuendo, phrasing choices, and tone of voice by counterparts in the client organization.

Whenever available, it can be good practice to show your personnel video tapes of meetings, especially of prior meetings with the client in question. Turning off the volume and asking viewers to observe and interpret non-verbal signals by the speakers can be a powerful training mechanism.

Similarly, after the meeting, you can repeat the video process, again asking what can be gleaned about participants' motives. It's also instructive to review which non-verbal signals your team members were able to identify properly and which were not.

Business Plan: The Business Plan is the detailed explanation or argument for how one intends to achieve success: "success" is defined in terms of explicit short-, medium-, and long-term objectives, logically connecting objectives to stated goal(s).

The Business Plan outlines necessary investments, dispersal timing (how and when resources will be required for personnel, property, plant and equipment, technology, marketing, research and development) and encompasses the Value Proposition for each identifiable target audience and market segment.

The Business Plan must demonstrate, in quantifiable terms, your vision for the rewards your individual and collective efforts will bring to investors and other stakeholders.

In the Business Plan, you must address anticipated industry and macroeconomic trends, competitor's expected moves and counter-moves, changes in regulatory environments and other risks candidly. The plan should reflect both your foresight and expertise.

If your goal is to increase revenues by 50% during the first year, a clear outline of how you will deploy the necessary resources and generate those revenues—whether by a combination of cost-cutting, increasing sales, bringing new products or services online, and/or selling unprofitable business lines for cash—your strategy must be stated in firm time lines, hard dollars and cents, and sound business reasoning that demonstrates your grasp of the business, the marketplace, and macroeconomic factors.

Savvy investors and bankers—the ones you want on your team—see dozens and dozens of Business Plans every quarter: the competition for investment and venture capital is exceedingly fierce. Use all the brains and talent at your disposal—include both the technical and managerial expertise available at every level in your firm and every professional network you can access—collaborate, question, dream, brainstorm, evaluate, test and prove every element of the Business Plan for efficiency and effectiveness.

Every initiative, project and business unit must have a plan: these plans must all link together (or "roll-up") to yield the overall, firm-level plan. Examples of plans that "roll up" include marketing plans, product engineering blueprints, as well as policy and procedure outlines. All must be relevant to the overall objectives, and all must be internally consistent.

Business environments are dynamic: obviously, successful business plans will necessarily change over time. Be flexible; as macroeconomic trends change, as you learn and the firm evolves, plans have to be refined and adjusted to meet both new opportunities and new risks.

Beware of changing your plans too frequently (monthly or quarterly); changing the over-all plan may require changes in the plan for each initiative, project, and business unit: no one would get anything done beyond constantly writing new plans.

Frequently revamping your business plan signals your lack of understanding of the business and the marketplace: truly *strategic* changes burn significant resources (management time, research, or revenues). Frequent strategy changes will be seen as just what they are: indecision. Indecision reduces faith in management, lowers morale, and accelerates staff departures.

Clearly, the first rule of writing a Business Plan parallels the first rule of risk management: know how your company is (not) working. Otherwise, you have no basis for writing a plan to correct what is not working. Researching your Business Plan is absolutely critical. The only possible way to gain a deep understanding of feasible and advisable moves is to look at everything and ask the hard question: do the firm's offerings synergize to supply compelling solutions?

The goal of the process is to ask the right questions, decide whether a "problem" is a "problem" or a *symptom* of a not-yet understood problem. Elicit the highest levels of creativity, most thoughtful discussions and "Aha!" moments from your staff. Everyone benefits from participation in wide-open exploration to probe company history, learn what patterns of behavior have been successful in business cycles, and consider how best to apply that knowledge, both short- and long-term.

However, not everyone will understand the difference between "exploration" and "finger-pointing." Not everyone knows how to be open-minded. Consider hiring an experienced mediator to lead the discussion, so you can truly participate and observe: staff should see that their skills and opinions count, that they are seen as part of the solution, not the problem.

Writing these plans is hard work, and requires the best input possible from experts, stakeholders, and the folks who are going to have to do the work. Generic plans don't work, but all good business plans have these elements in common:

- Identify where you need to be, in terms of people and processes, to be successful; define "success."

- Take the causes of distress identified in your earlier investigations into full account;

- Scrutinize every plan element to avoid unintended consequences;

- Set realistic timelines.

The challenge, of course, is realistic appraisal and pragmatic choices. Pixie dust, superstitious rituals, or the business equivalent of rain dancing may lighten the discussions, but do not qualify as solid plan elements.

Focus is required in planning for any firm, but especially for an ailing one. Some areas requiring focus are discussed below:

Many companies stretch themselves too thinly when they are trying to grow. They may become involved in myriad, superficially-related businesses or markets with no compelling synergies. Opening too many new offices or branches is a classic error, and a frequently false signal of success: new offices mean more overhead costs, potential language and culture challenges, and more opportunities to lose focus. The new locations create more physical separation between staff, communications degrade and the power of the *esprit de corps* that binds the survivors of the bad times together is lessened or lost.

It's tempting to continue a variety of business activities, especially when it is uncertain which ones will be most successful; hanging on to business lines or divisions as an effective hedge against uncertainty can be a symptom of indecisive planning. It's legitimate to hedge wherever possible, but you have limited resources. You must maintain discipline and avoid spreading those resources too thinly. Non-core businesses must be discontinued; if you can sell them off for cash, so much the better.

One of the most important words you as a manager must be able to use judiciously is "No." No to bad plans; no to poor performance; no to politically motivated ideas. A tightly written Mission Statement empowers you and other managers to say "No" to suggestions that conflict with your Mission. Strong Business Plans and solid Value Propositions give management an objective basis for making the "Yes/No" decision on any matter.

Issues Affecting Planning

Constraints limiting a manager's freedom are the inescapable reality of corporate life; they are more numerous and bind more tightly in a troubled firm already trailing the competition.

Here are some issues, considerations, and constraints you can expect:

The Clock Is Ticking

Time is a matter of perspective: it either seems to rush by, or drags so slowly we cannot believe our eyes when we look at the clock. As a manager charged with a turnaround, you will most frequently find yourself with your limited time speeding past.

As soon as your appointment as the new executive is announced, clocks start ticking, and they will not all be synchronized with yours!

Both clients and staff begin forming expectations, including the time they will allot you to tackle their problems. The problems *clients* consider their worst bother them most; they will ask about them first, and expect you to solve them first. You may not see their concern as requiring immediate attention and want to exercise some patience, take the time to investigate the problem, and act reasonably. Unfortunately, their "wake up and do something, *anything, now!*" alarms are clanging. Sometimes you must engage them immediately, lest the din become so distracting your own schedules suffer.

Acknowledge troublesome issues: bring them into the open as your first formal acts; staff, clients, and partners will appreciate the validation. They may even shut off the alarms long enough to let you hear yourself think.

The length of time needed to seek and reach a timely resolution will depend on the scope and scale of the challenge; the intensity of the external or internal demand for a solution may, or may not, be proportional to the demand.

However, the most important clock is yours: do not allow your calendar to be hijacked; maintain control of time even at the risk of offending others; do the right things, at the right time.

Austerity Measures

Austerity measures are often the first necessary turnaround steps. Austerity measures, in this context, refer to *extreme* cost-cutting you must do to keep the firm afloat in the near-term: austerity measures are required only after obvious reductions to bloated payrolls, expensive perks, exorbitant bonuses, and other excessive expenditures fail to stanch the red-ink flow.

Bringing the net (revenue minus expenses) under control may give you and your management team time to set the next phases of recovery in motion, to move away from cost-cutting to ensuring that your revenues are on a healthy trajectory. Recovery means fixing the firm's products, revisiting Value Propositions, building or re-educating a sales force, and generating new revenues from new sources according to your Business Plan.

No one likes austerity measures: they are tolerable *only* when finite. Austerity measures require rigorous self-discipline, strict adherence to budgets, and are downright inconvenient. Austerity measures that require staff to temporarily curtail their discretionary spending is a dramatic psychological reminder that times are bad. Maintaining unity under the pressure of such severe discipline requires your charisma, personal credibility and sound, transparent plans the staff can *believe* are necessary to save the company and lead it to solvency. Your plans must set reasonable time lines: if months drag into years, their faith in you and a brighter future will diminish.

Cost-cutting and austerity can be part of the right answer, but not the only answer: a new leader who decides that the only necessary measures to fix the firm are to cut costs by reducing travel budgets, hiring freezes, or replacing sales forces is more than likely making some poor decisions.

Cutting costs is simple, but rarely addresses the true causes of a firm's dysfunction; lower expenses may increase profitability, but typically only in the short-term. If your plans call for cost-cutting only, only symptoms are being addressed. The root causes of the firm's problems remain hidden: failure to address the systemic dysfunction will eventually be revealed, and will (and should) cost the leader his job.

Staff already knows the company is in trouble: some cost-cutting measures are probably already in place. However, "cost-cutting," in comparison to the poorly-controlled spending that got the company in trouble in the first place, may just be realistic spending. True austerity is more serious. You have to *sell* austerity measures: matters of this import require you to *stand up* in front of your people, ideally in the same room.

Tell them the unvarnished truth, in sufficient detail for them to understand the company's fiscal state.

Propose your ultimate goals for the company. Explain how you set the goals and why you concluded austerity measures are necessary. If they are to agree with your logic, concede to *temporary* austerity measures, and cooperate in reaching the desired goals, you must be forthright and tell them how long the painful concessions must be borne. Give them the "best case" and "worst case" timelines; if the turnaround takes longer because of circumstances beyond anyone's control, the actual timeline will still be within their range of expectations.

Cost-cutting measures require balancing the time necessary to allow the firm financial breathing room against the duration of the staff's tolerance before they rebel. Widespread rebellion may spell the end of the turnaround effort—perhaps the end of the firm.

Austerity measures are never easy to sell; however, the state of the overall economy and job markets are important factors. If you are cutting paychecks and perks during a hot job market, expect high attrition as employees quickly seek alternative employment. If job markets are weak, available alternatives are less compelling, and you have a greater chance to retain staff, at least in the near-term. Regardless, even draconian measures must be finite and fair.

It's Lonely at the Top

The saying, "It's lonely at the top" is very true: becoming too- personally involved in any relationship, project, decision, or plan risks clouded judgment and muddled planning.

Your hardest decisions will disappoint some people. Making the critical, painful decisions that affect people's careers and livelihoods require the courage of clarity: if the company is to survive, some competent people may be demoted, or lose their jobs.

Company survival also requires firing people who have demonstrated their incompetence, stolen property or money, created hostile work environments. The courage of clarity requires that you dismiss them cleanly, "for cause" you have carefully documented.

Sympathy and righteous anger are perfectly appropriate emotional reactions in dealing with these two groups of people: maintaining dignity, however, requires that you treat both groups as adults who must be told painful truths, calmly, without remorse or rancor. You may really like the embezzler—a funny, smart, nice guy: but he's still an embezzler.

Some degree of detachment may also be appropriate in dealing with your bosses, too: a member of the Board or another senior executive may champion a project that has been "his baby" from startup, but no longer fits the firm's core business. Choosing to divert resources to more urgent projects may be very unpopular, but you would breach your fiduciary duty to the firm if you failed to write the Business Plan to make "highest and best use" of limited resources.

It is legitimate to formulate plans that follow a path of least resistance *only* when the outcome is the best possible for the firm: "least resistance" cannot include your personal considerations.

Example: *Several years ago I came into a turnaround situation involving a unit of about 100 people, within a much larger organization of several thousand. An immediate observation was that one of the smaller unit's Managing Directors (MD) had been leading a money-losing department for several years, yet consistently received hefty annual bonuses.*

Careful investigation revealed that the MD in question had a very strong friendship with one of the firm's Executive Vice Presidents (EVPs), dating back twenty years when the two had joined the firm together as junior Associates. Further investigation revealed widespread opinions among staff members that the MD had benefited over the years from this powerful friend, despite lacking credentials and experience.

Evaluating the MD's performance made it quickly and painfully clear that he was significantly lacking appropriate skills for the job.

It also became clear that over the years, the MD's managers, always aware of his powerful friend, had decided to provide overly-favorable annual reviews. Thus, the MD was never given candid feedback, had an unrealistic view of his own abilities, and had been deprived of opportunities to address skill limitations, because he'd never been made aware of them. His department, meanwhile, had suffered significantly over the years, losing millions of dollars, as well as a number of promising staff members who'd left in disgust.

While the EVP undoubtedly thought he was loyally helping his friend, he had actually done nothing of the sort. He'd let his friend down by depriving him of opportunities to develop much-needed skills, and more important, had failed in his duty to the firm by allowing poor leadership and management to persist, with tangible costs.

End note: When the dust settled on the turnaround effort, the MD's department was placed under someone else's care. The MD's day-to-day activities were assigned to an entry–level junior Associate, who was able to handle them quite capably. The MD still landed on his feet. When the EVP heard the turnaround reviews and recommendations, he couldn't resist one final act of "kindness," insisting that his friend retain his MD title and be given a similarly inflated role in another division of the firm.

Global Considerations

We are all doing business in our globally integrated and interconnected world, whether we recognize it or not: you must know enough about the rest of the world to ensure you know explicitly when and where globalization benefits—or harms—your company.

Plans that do not take into account geographically distant players who are potentially formidable competitors, or technological advances being developed in other markets that could be useful to your firm, demonstrate ignorance of globalization. Ignorance is, fortunately, a curable condition.

Lucrative markets, better partners, suppliers and financing opportunities may be awaiting discovery on the other side of the world (or just over the horizon, or down the block.) Ignorance of the existing and potential sources of your raw materials, product components, hardware and software, and any other business element or tool always puts you at an immediate disadvantage, because you cannot anticipate or calculate the probabilities that political risk, violence, transportation disruption, labor strikes, natural disasters or any of the other risks will damage your business.

Every company of significant size must have access to experts, either as consultants or on staff, who fully understand how to navigate the complex international aspects of day-to-day business and short- and long-term planning. Troubled firms searching for new markets, suppliers, and partners have even more urgent reasons to seek sound counsel about global realities and considerations.

People are central to your global capabilities:

- Hire emotionally competent, multilingual staff with excellent communications skills;

- Hire individuals from diverse ethnic, geographic and social backgrounds;

- Expose *everyone* to *mandatory* cultural sensitivity training;

- Attend international forums relevant to your field;

- Have your people step outside day-to-day routines and observe what the rest of the world is doing.

    A. Urge them to initiate travel plans or take advantage of existing itineraries to visit other regions and countries.

B. Have them make an effort to interact with people outside their normal circles.

C. Encourage them to peruse magazines, books and newspapers that are not part of their daily routines.

- Consider whether your processes (back, middle, and front office) can be divided and handled more effectively and efficiently in different regions.

- Consider whether you can become an outsourcer for other firms domiciled in the next state or in far-off lands. Ask yourself what would make those other firms want to outsource some of their operations to your firm.

- Consider how ideas, strategies, tactics, wisdom, and expertise can be shared across offices.

Assuming that just because a company has a few offices around the world it's "global" is laughable: mere physical presence in multiple locations without tapping the best locations and skills to envision, design, test, build, market, sell and support your offerings does not make your firm "global."

Where are your headquarters? A truly "global" entity does not subscribe to the traditional concept of a single headquarters with satellite offices in other countries: that model already misses the point. A truly global enterprise operates a worldwide network of interrelated and symbiotic assets, and leverages them to service a global audience. There is no distinct headquarters, only a network of interconnected functional and support groups spanning the globe.

Macroeconomic Considerations

Existing and expected macroeconomic trends are complex, difficult to predict, and dangerous when misunderstood. No struggling firm can hope to survive, much less thrive, without thoroughly understanding macroeconomic realities.

Questions that must be answered during the planning stages:

- How do GDP, oil prices, interest rates, and foreign exchange rates affect the firm's businesses?

- What are the most realistic trend projections for each of these factors?

- Does the anticipated macroeconomic environment provide good or bad prospects for the firm's current offerings suite?

- Is it necessary to re-engineer or completely re-think some or all of the firm's offerings?

- Should the firm's finance function hedge to reduce the risks of adverse moves in macroeconomic indicators?

In addition, every Business Plan must contemplate the firm's "Plan B" when "Plan A" no longer works due to "unanticipated consequences" of market and financial trends.

Research & Development Plans

Research & Development (R&D) plans determine the investment the firm makes to generate innovations that fuel future offerings; R&D planning is especially challenging for a distressed firm where long-term plans must be subservient to near-term survival. There often just isn't enough funding "left over" for R&D, based on the logic that there will be no long-term for the firm unless near-term cost-cuts save the company. Over time, such firms find themselves at greater and greater disadvantage compared to firms that maintained their commitment to R&D, cut costs elsewhere, and invested in innovation.

Correct choices about how much, where, and when to spend limited resources distinguish visionary leaders from mediocre ones. Answering the hard questions about R&D requires clarity: are you, or are you not, leader enough to calculate the risks and decide how much future to sacrifice for marginal survival advantages in the near-term? You signed on for the "big bucks" and the corner office: these decisions are where you earn them.

Each situation presents its own complexities, and you were hired to exercise your common sense, best judgment, and business experience. Common sense and business experience support the argument that when a company is on the brink of extinction with wake-up alarms clanging and the hands on the very long-term clock hardly moving, dedicating available resources to immediate survival seems to be a good judgment call. Again, you still have to decide how much future you are willing to sacrifice for marginal survival advantages in the near-term.

Short-term or even emergency borrowing may be necessary. The company's financial condition may make traditional lenders shy away; consider all possible lending sources, and have your Business Plan well-polished. If you have a parent company, convincing the leaders that strategic investment is critical to realizing significant rewards in the long-term is an excellent survival plan.

External investors willing to take some ownership in return for investment dollars are another source of survival: your clarity and courage to drive a hard-enough bargain to protect your company's present and future from corporate raiders in investors' clothing is required.

Circumstances Shape Perceptions and Expectations

Coming in to any new environment where you are expected to wield authority makes you the subject of intense scrutiny; everyone wants to know about you, regardless of whether you are replacing a beloved leader, are an insider or outsider, have a strong track record or are being given your first shot at senior management. Do not underestimate the power of circumstances in shaping people's perceptions and expectations.

Replacing a Beloved Leader: This is often the most challenging environment because many observers believe that no one can fill those "big shoes" they have placed on a pedestal, and will constantly compare your ideas and plans to the approach they assume your predecessor would have preferred, whether or not their assumptions are correct. Some may believe that giving you any opportunity to succeed is "disloyal," or is not respectful of "the old man's" legacy. Accept that you may never replace your predecessor in the hearts of "his" people; your plans will be scrutinized in light of your predecessor's assumed, possibly known, strategy and aspirations. You will be second-guessed, criticized, and treated as an interloper unless/until you earn their (grudging) loyalty and respect by exercising enough emotional competence and business acumen to improve the company.

Insider versus Outsider: An "insider" in a distressed firm is likely to be viewed negatively. The company has problems, *ergo* management must be doing something wrong, *ergo* what is the point of appointing someone who only knows the *status quo* and may be guilty, by omission or commission, of contributing to the distress?

An "outsider" may be viewed as a breath of fresh air, or met with greater suspicion because she is an unknown quantity. "The evil that we know is best" (Titus Maccius Plautus 254 – 184 BCE) is a common reaction from individuals who find *any* change threatening, regardless of the potential for benefit or damage.

Experienced versus Inexperienced: Predictably, your reception will be warmer if you have a proven track record. People in a distressed firm will be more inclined to give you the benefit of the doubt when you've been in these situations before, and succeeded. If this is your first senior posting, the staff may be concerned about your (untried) ability to lead them, and more reluctant to accept your plans, especially if they seem too ambitious or bold.

Identical plans proposed by an executive who follows a beloved leader, one who is an "insider" or "outsider," with experience or without, will be judged in light of biases "for" or "against" each circumstance: be mindful that your ability to persuade others to follow you long enough for you to earn their respect and loyalty is your over-riding task.

Staff Members' Predispositions

When you first arrive, you are an unknown,. People will test you consciously and subconsciously for tangible and intangible leadership and management skills. These tests will lead to snap judgments in turnaround situations where everyone is on edge and desperately seeking competent leadership.

First impressions are lasting: very few people—even accomplished actors—can fool an interested observer. Studies at Harvard University confirm that impressions from the first 30 seconds of meeting someone are lasting: observers' impressions are accurate about *80 percent of the time*.

The initial impressions and snap judgments by staff will set the tone of your tenure. Some will "test" you by asking questions with some preconceived notion of what the "correct" answers are. The questioners will explore whether your ultimate plan is to rescue the firm only, "the employees be damned." They have a legitimate interest in knowing whether you genuinely care about them, are committed to their emotional well-being, personal satisfaction, and financial success. If an incumbent manager and/or his decisions are disliked or considered incompetent, the questions may be directed at discovering your leanings—toward the employees, or the manager. Questioners and observers will weigh your words, your facial expression, your body language and gestures carefully, seeking hidden meaning. Your decisions will be closely examined, your actions carefully judged.

Your honesty and sincerity will work in your favor; reserving judgment is a respectable option, provided you clearly explain your thoughts. Be prepared for very one-sided expectations: either you are there to help, or you're there to fire everyone. If the staff believe you are able and inclined to succeed, they will breathe a sigh of relief, give you the benefit of their doubts, and support you. If they believe you are more of the same bad medicine they have experienced in the past, their morale will drop further, along with any inclination to cooperate with you, regardless of the genius of your plans.

Best case scenario: the majority of the people will see you as honest and capable, and will voluntarily support you and your plans. There will be internal disagreements about decisions that must be made: 100% agreement in any group of thinking individuals is rare. Most people will conclude your arrival is a positive event, others will, undoubtedly, see it as a negative outcome.

A manager finding himself in this situation may want to win (all) people over by telling them what he thinks they want to hear. The problems are:

- There isn't a single consistent message that will please everyone;

- He may not yet fully understand what each person wants to hear, and what they want to hear may not be the most constructive path forward.

- It's often not possible, so early on, to provide specifics as to how you should proceed.

- Have confidence in your ability to make good decisions: take actions because you believe they are the correct moves for your constituents (employees, shareholders, the Board, etc.), not because you are consciously or subconsciously seeking to please others.

- The eternal pessimists, who will guarantee your failure, stand at the negative end of the spectrum; those who see you as the long-awaited leader stand at the other, while most of the staff and managers will be strung along the spectrum between the two extremes.

You may like to think that everyone will judge you on your merits: usually, the extremists on both ends of the spectrum are not reacting to your skills—they are reflecting their own personalities. In other words, regardless of the skills you, or any other manager, portray, the pessimists will be pessimists and the optimists will be optimists. Those holding more centrist views tend to be more objective; they are the important ones to win over. In some sense, they are the middle class "swing vote" you will need to sell your platform to, and get their support.

Set Realistic Priorities

Most likely, you won't have too much difficulty identifying some necessary changes: the problem will be to decide which to pursue first, second, third, and whether to revise the order when you realize the *problem* you were addressing is really a *symptom*. Your preferred plan will undoubtedly also be limited due to resource constraints. You must opt for actions that yield the greatest impact for the firm.

Priorities depend greatly on your planning horizon: if you are focused on surviving for one more financial quarter, you will likely make very different decisions than if you had the luxury of planning for a three-year horizon. The choice of horizon may be out of your control; it may depend on external macroeconomic factors, or Board preferences, or depth of the owners' pockets.

Setting *correct* priorities is critical because resource scarcities mean *only* the top priorities—those most likely to lower costs and increase revenues—can be funded: anything below the top of the list is likely to be wishful thinking.

When you come across a process that is working, even if somewhat imperfectly, consider leaving it alone for the moment: the issue can always be revisited later, while in the near-term you can move on to other more pressing needs. *Your Business Plan should reflect the decision to leave certain items or processes as they are, along with a statement of intent to return to these items when time and funding permit.*

Risks

Plans must also fully account for potential risks. Risks come in many forms, including:

- *Credit Risk:* The possibility that money owed by a counterparty will not be paid back.

- *Market Risk:* The possibility that the value of investments or assets will move in an unfavorable direction.

- *Reputation Risk:* The possibility that an unfavorable event will harm the firm's brand name in the marketplace.

- *Operational Risk:* The risk that human errors or shortcoming in processes will lead to losses.

- *Natural Disaster Risk:* The risk that fire, earthquake, or flood will disrupt the firm's activities.

Quantifying risks can be very useful in planning. Having a more concrete sense of the extent of potential losses reduces the uncertainty and makes risk mitigation more precise.

Not only should all relevant risks be considered in formulation of Business Plans, there should be special risk management plans available in the event that extreme risks are realized. As an example, it's vitally important for a firm to have emergency contingency plans ready ahead of time to deal with natural disasters.

Due to neglect and distraction, troubled firms tend to have poorer risk management awareness and often will not have any contingency plans in place.

Your Business Plan must embrace and plan for risks necessary to its business, and avoid those that do not belong to the core business. For example, if you are not a financial institution, avoid trying to extend credit to clients in innovative ways: your company most likely does not have the experience and infrastructure to manage credit risk. If your firm produces natural resources, consider leaving commodity speculation (market trading risks) to others; remove these risks using readily available instruments such as futures contracts.

Expectations

Individual and collective expectations determine, to a great degree, whether people are encouraged or discouraged with a particular outcome. The key for you, as manager, is to understand people's existing expectations, and positively influence their expectations by clearly communicating your policies and intentions as soon as they are formulated.

The failure to manage expectations is one of the greatest failings of management, causing, or deepening, a firm's distress. The failure typically comes about for several reasons:

- Management is unaware their actions or inactions are creating particular expectations; failure to anticipate reactions, and/or failure to read staff behavior, is clearly a function of lack of empathy and political awareness.

- Management is aware of expectations but believes they are realistic, when in reality they are not.

- Management is aware that expectations are not in line with reality, but is too concerned about the immediate repercussions of a public admission of financial troubles or scandal to understand the true impact of the disconnect between expectations and reality. Occasionally, there is a hope (or a prayer) that in time, some significant event (a miracle) will arise, allowing the original expectations to be met.

Unrealistic (inflated) expectations cause anxiety for all concerned: it is challenging to meet inflated expectations in any setting; in a turnaround situation it's viciously difficult, particularly when management is so unaware of staff attitudes they have no accurate measures of staff will and capacity to meet goals.

When compensation is tied to performance expectations, the inability to meet (unrealistic) goals will quickly lead to departures at a critical time, and completely undermine the turnaround effort.

The Mission Statement, Business Plan, and Value Propositions written in clear, incisive language are believable because they reflect deep understanding of the risks and rewards contemplated in the turnaround effort—establish realistic expectations among internal constituencies (staff, senior management, and the Board) and external constituencies (clients, prospects, external shareholders, partners, suppliers and lenders).

Example: A new leader came into a firm which had two units of comparable size; one delivered consulting services and one produced and marketed products.

In his first speech to staff, he stated: "I'm a consultant. I don't know much about product development and management, and frankly, I don't have much use for it. My only prior experience was with an expensive product, which had to be terminated after steep losses."

The immediate effect of this ill-conceived speech was a polarized staff.

The consulting group were elated; here was a person fashioned in their mold.

The product group were shocked; their common interpretation was that they would all be fired, with, perhaps, a few "lucky" ones offered some role in the consulting group—which interested none of them.

The entire sequence reflects very poorly on the new "leader"; he left a first impression of arrogance, contempt, and vanity—he was never able to overcome the damage done.

Perhaps this individual felt he was "managing expectations," as he certainly made his intentions clear. However, the Board who hired him apparently did not make their intentions clear. It is hard to imagine an interview process that did not reveal the "leader's" very narrow comfort zone, nor how discussions of the firm's Mission Statement, Business Plan, or Value Propositions did not uncover how quickly this clearly emotionally incompetent individual's vision would alienate half the firm.

The Board, to its credit, apparently recognized their horrific error in judgment and replaced the "leader" after less than a year.

Plan for Early "Wins"

That first "win" is critical to employee morale and your company's reputation in the marketplace. A "win" is a positive development: successful rollout of a new product, a sale to a strategically-important client, agreement by a client to have their firm's name included in a press release, hiring a good candidate, removing a much-hated process.

The win need not be a huge success. Realistically, struggling firms don't magically come up with huge wins out of thin air. But they are able to realize small wins which can halt the negative momentum and eventually build positive momentum.

CHAPTER 8
Turn Your People Around

The most critical element of the turnaround is to attend to your people: set fair, equitable employment policies; evaluate incumbents' performance, recruit and hire new/replacement employees, develop and promote staff, and, when necessary, terminate employment of those who cannot, or will not, contribute to the company's success.

In a very small company, you may manage these functions yourself. In a larger firm, you should have a human resources (HR) function to charge with implementing and supporting people-related changes necessary to putting the firm on a healthy path.

Recruiting and hiring people who exhibit the "Top Twelve" traits (self-disciplined individuals with a strong work ethic, demonstrated integrity and proven technical skill) is a beginning. Balancing recruiting and hiring with developing incumbents, while supporting a corporate culture and overall environment that does not encourage the appearance, or strengthening, of the Dirty Dozen traits requires full-time, professional attention.

Demonstrate that people truly are your most important asset: first, invest in the best human resource professionals available. Unfortunately, too many companies' HR departments are an afterthought, their staff considered second-class citizens—until there is a hiring crisis, or an employee-related lawsuit, or a nasty labor dispute.

Considering HR professionals less important than the firm's professional engineers, consultants, or salespeople is a gross error in judgment: capable HR staff can make the difference between success and failure of *any* company, particularly a distressed one. Any company whose management takes a dismissive attitude towards the HR function is hurting its own present and future. A distressed company that dismisses HR functions is committing corporate suicide.

Employment and civil rights laws, requirements for hiring qualified minorities and women, and equal pay for equal work laws have been on federal and state books for more than forty years: the need for competent HR staff is "old news."

The disdain directed at HR roles often begins with management who long for the (possibly existent only in urban myth) "good old days" when payroll clerks could manage most of the compliance issues, as they were generally withholding-tax-related. Owner-managers who still resent the (increasing) need for staff/overhead costs to comply with local, state and federal employment laws are demonstrating their own failure to recognize and manage legitimate risks. The penalties for ignoring (or simply failing to comply with) employment, Employment Retirement Income Security Act (ERISA), and employee safety laws can be very expensive.

HR personnel are especially important during periods of turmoil or uncertainty: every event takes on greater meaning for employees. Human nature dictates at least some employees will assign sinister meaning to messages from management, regardless of whether there is objective reason for such interpretation. Occurrences that normally wouldn't lead people to bat an eyelash suddenly turn into public displays of aggression, recriminations, and even lawsuits.

Example: *Several years ago, a middle manager approached me with a confidential issue. He'd been providing feedback to an employee in a one-on-one setting. The two had a long, very solid friendship as colleagues. Over the most recent year, the firm had been performing quite poorly. Competitors had managed to win over some long-time clients, and there had been a need to terminate some employees' employment. Thinking he was acting responsibly, he gave the employee positive feedback, as well as some thoughts about how the employee could do a better job by being more proactive around the office, and, in particular, assisting him during peak load periods, which would require her staying in the office a bit later once or twice a week. The employee reacted strongly to this feedback and, to make a long story short, implied that his suggestions were an inappropriate advance.*

Anyone who'd known the two would have been utterly surprised at the allegation. Both were married, happily, and had, at all times, exhibited respectful behavior to each other, as well as everyone else in the office.

The next day the manager approached me again, visibly relieved; he explained that the employee had come in early and apologized for the earlier allegation. She'd explained that her reaction had resulted from the increasingly stressful office environment; she had been overcome with a feeling that management was seeking reasons to fire people.

This story had a good ending, but in many cases managers and employees find themselves swept along an unintended path due to strained circumstances. Fortunately, in this instance, the collegial relationship between the two people in question was strong enough to withstand a shock; however, the manager could have done a better job of recognizing his colleague's stress, and chosen his words more carefully to ensure his feedback did not add to already-heightened anxiety.

Having HR professionals to intervene, defuse, or mediate the impact of shocking, emotionally incompetent behavior is critical as you struggle to mend relationships, build bridges, and right the ship.

The subsequent discussion in this chapter is directed to you, as the top manager, but doesn't necessarily mean you must personally perform or oversee each of the recommended actions. Taking an active interest is useful: the value in HR professionals executing employment policy while you wrestle with other, pressing problems is your peace of mind, at least about employment issues.

If you concluded that your senior HR manager is technically and emotionally competent, empower him to clarify roles and responsibilities for all employees as soon as they are formulated, and distribute the written policy and procedures promptly. HR is responsible for implementing and consistently following recruiting and hiring, retention, training, development, and termination processes.

Clarity

Establish clear roles and responsibilities consistent with the Mission Statement, Business Plan and Value Propositions: begin with senior executives and work all the way through the organization to entry-level positions. Clarifying authority and responsibilities is urgent: HR is the natural lead in the overhaul. Project deliverables include:

- Policy statement clarifying how personnel will support the Mission Statement and Business Plan;

- Precise job descriptions for all roles, with detailed explanation of authority, duties and responsibilities, including behavioral expectations consistent with required emotional competencies for each functional and support position;

- Delineation of responsibilities. Where does one person's responsibility end and another's begin? Flexible guidelines for collaborative decision-making, single-project team decision-making, and accepting or declining internal or external recommendations to facilitate initiative and innovation; particularly when units are reorganized, or mergers bring overlapping functions together.

- Policies regarding when, why, and by whom assigning or delegating authority is appropriate: *authority may be delegated, ultimate responsibility cannot.*

- Clear statement of hierarchical structure and managerial oversight, particularly when mergers or acquisitions have yet to be fully integrated, or are planned.

- Well understood, reliable lines of communication that take official, interim, and unofficial reporting patterns into consideration.

- Quantifiable, transparent definitions of success and measures of individual (and unit) progress.

- Clear performance expectations, tracking and reviews for each role/person, each sub-unit, and the entire firm.

- Overall corporate growth expectations (if relevant).

- Personal growth expectations.

- A transparent methodology outlining how financial compensation is determined, when and how regular paychecks are distributed, and when and how rewards for exceptional performance are paid.

Once everyone is clear how their work fits into the overall Mission Statement and Business Plan, personnel goals embodied in individual and team performance plans that underlie and support the company vision are simpler to understand and follow. Set clear goals with your direct reports: integrate the setting of consistent goals with direct reports at every company level into performance and compensation plans.

Skepticism and reluctance to change and fit into *any* newer, more transparent system is natural. Instill the vision that naturally narrows focus for maximum clarity: articulate the strategy and repeat it until everyone understands the overarching priorities and task(s) at hand.

Adjust/Align Incentives

Setting clear, consistent (and realistic) goals isn't enough to motivate everyone. Strategy and intent can be explained endlessly, but setting incentives *meaningful* to individuals and teams is an excellent motivator.

Institute a Rewards System: Design systems that reinforce the firm's values. Financial goals, production objectives, market penetration and/or community service are reward elements that recognize support for co-workers, and contribute to positive work environments, boldness and risk-taking. Encourage pro-bono work; "loan" executives to public service and charitable organizations to head annual fund drives while keeping the executives on your payroll.

Accelerate Rewards as Contributions to Success Increase: Pay everyone who meets a sales target a 100% bonus or commission; pay those who exceed the goal an additional bonus, say 120% for some extended target, perhaps as much as 150% bonus for the top producer.

Consider production goals in every setting, and quantify their economic value to your firm. Production at entry-level clerical or machine operator positions, where tasks are relatively simple, is very measurable. One noted study, by John Hunter, University of Michigan, and his University of Iowa colleagues Frank Schmidt and Michael Judiesch, found that the output of the *top one percent* was about *three times the output of the bottom one percent:* clearly, an individual producing three times more than another should be paid accordingly.

Support functions may seem less amenable to measurement, but consider human resources: the individual who recruits the largest number of highly-qualified candidates, within a specific time limit, is *selling* the company as effectively as the top sales producer, and deserves the same compensation considerations.

Reward people for new product or process ideas; recognize their desire to contribute beyond their assigned tasks with cash, or rewards such as theater tickets or gift certificates. If/when their ideas survive rigorous validation, additional reward is in order. If the product is approved and goes into production, a cash bonus and the opportunity to participate in marketing or managing the product is reasonable.

Acknowledging individual and team effort when patents are granted to the company is very satisfying to R&D staff.

Offer People a Stake in the Firm: Awarding equity—stock shares, or discounts on stock purchases—is one proven way to impart immediacy to long-term goals. People who recognize the relationship between today's choices and long-term profitability make better choices.

Tailor Incentives to Roles: Sales people may be motivated by commission-based compensation directly related to units sold and revenue generated: competitive individuals like to "keep score." A product manager may find a year-end bonus more motivating.

Recognize researchers with longer-term (perhaps multi-year) bonus or equity plans that consider the time necessary to bring an idea through applied research and product development to earning revenue.

Tailor Incentives to Individuals: Insisting that everyone in a particular function accept the same compensation/rewards system in a misguided attempt to "level the playing field" misses the point of emotional competency in leadership.

Conventional wisdom may dictate that all sales staff be aggressive hard drivers for whom commission-based compensation is an incentive; when the objective is to increase revenue, or overtake the competition, commission-driven paychecks make sense.

However, when the objective is to maintain significant accounts and only marginal new sales to existing clients are expected, a base salary with periodic bonuses for client retention may be more reasonable.

Small company leaders may not believe they can accommodate salespeople in both roles. Weighing the risk/cost of losing an outstanding sales representative because living from commission-to-commission would be adverse to his family, versus a "fast burner" with only short-term financial goals, is worth the time and attention to fully consider hiring/retention decisions.

There are some individuals to whom the whole notion of chasing bonuses or participating in internal competition is distracting and demeaning. Do not expect to change their perspective: it is a result of their deepest nature. These individuals may be motivated by the pleasure of producing exceptionally high-quality work for its own sake. When you identify such people, seek to agree on a mutually beneficial compensation mechanism, allowing them to focus on productivity. Your company will reap the rewards of your excellent judgment.

Tie compensation to the behavior you desire. When you get it right it's like magic; people willingly cooperate. Get it wrong, and it feels like you're herding cats.

No matter how hard you try, and how much thought you put into incentives, the Law of Unintended Consequences will rear its ugly head. Perfect sets of interlocking incentives don't come in boxes; you have to build them out of the same raw materials you use to create Mission Statements and Business Plans—thoughtful analysis of Best Practices, hard data applied correctly, and good business sense.

Refine or change incentives, over time, to reflect the demographic changes in your own employee populations, stock market and other macroeconomic changes, mergers and acquisitions. Regular, frequent employee performance evaluations are the best time to gauge the effectiveness of incentive mechanisms. Be proactive in renegotiating them as necessary to preserve the critical core of human capital.

Recruiting and Hiring

Many volumes have been written about recruiting; *Topgrading*, by Bradford Smart, is particularly useful. I will discuss a few highlights relevant to finding and hiring emotionally- and technically-competent people.

Be very selective in your hiring decisions. Even if you have not yet integrated the concepts of employees as assets into your personal management philosophy, recognize the pure *financial cost* of hiring errors.

Ask yourself what your experience was like when you were interviewing for your current position. Did HR personnel and procedures play a positive, or negative, role in the process?

Recruiting requires at least these steps:

- Identifying positions which must be filled and the skills required for those positions;

- Casting a wide net to identify a deep pool of prospects;

- Putting candidates through a well-thought out and rigorous selection process;

- Showing the firm to best advantage to ensure the best candidates will want to join your enterprise.

Your HR team is responsible for working with existing personnel to create the needed job descriptions and associated skill requirements. The recruiters will use the myriad talent-search options available today efficiently and effectively. The Internet, traditional postings in newspapers and professional journals, professional networks, and external recruiters (headhunters) are all immediately available recruiting resources.

Broad commitment from staff to ensure qualified, consistent, and enthusiastic interviewers meeting with and screening candidates chosen from the pre-qualified lists is required. Searches for the right individuals in any labor market can be exhausting. Goleman discusses a recent survey of employers found that only about 19% of applicants possess sufficient self-discipline to succeed at an entry-level position. That's right: *nineteen percent.*

Obviously, finding qualified candidates is challenging enough: creating a sufficiently positive opinion of your firm to motivate them to accept an offer of employment requires the highest level of emotional competence in HR management, interviewers and support staff.

Recruiting and hiring good people is the goal in any company; it is *critical* in a troubled one, because new hires will often have to be thrown into action quickly, and survive and thrive under challenging conditions. Making the wrong hiring choice will mean having to repeat much of the recruiting process, draining scarce resources further.

Example: *An employee responsible for making technical decisions regarding whether billings are, or are not, payable and approving invoices for payment quits without notice, leaving stacks of documents with little or no action taken, incomprehensible notes, incomplete records, and thousands of dollars expended but unaccounted for during a period of a few months. There are no other similar positions in the firm. The manager lacks the technical skills to straighten out the mess (a clue to why an incompetent employee was able to last so long...) and internal auditors have reviewed only a sampling of transactions, chosen by the departed employee, nine months before quitting.*

Is the departed employee the problem, or a symptom of a management failure? Do you replace the departed employee, the manager, both, or restructure the process? Do you hire an outside consultant to fix the mess, then decide the qualifications necessary to fulfill the functions of the position(s)? Implement new internal auditing requirements?

The HR department must deliver a detailed, written plan outlining the hiring process:

- Specifying the basic information required from applicants;

- Which people within the company will lead the interviews (and why);

- Experience, training, or guidance required for non-HR interviewers before they evaluate a candidate's technical and emotional competencies;

- How many and what types of references may be required, and how those references are verified and evaluated;

- How feedback is collected from interviewers and compiled; and,

- How final candidates are chosen and decisions made to issue job offers.

Recruiters must consider whether a candidate:

- Is sufficiently skilled to perform the core duties of the role. Does she already possess the skills and/or can she gain them quickly?

- Is genuinely interested. Is the candidate merely using your firm as leverage against an offer from another firm or simply trying to get a raise from her current employer?

- Is sufficiently mature. Does the candidate have sufficient professional and/or life experience to judge her own capabilities fairly?

- Is resilient. Has she had to overcome adversity, or suffered a career setback? Did she come back stronger and wiser?

- Has the tenacity to commit to your cause. Does it appear she has the inner drive and discipline to stay the course?

- Is enthusiastic and possesses a sense of humor. Will she fit in well with her colleagues and contribute to a positive atmosphere?

- Is inclined to be a team player. Will she support her colleagues and contribute to a collaborative environment?

Rocking the boat a bit can help test candidates' interest, poise, and true demeanor. It's important to know how people will react to stress in the workplace, so it makes sense to push them a bit during interviews.

Recruiters are responsible for screening candidates for Top Twelve and Dirty Dozen traits during every interview, while checking, verifying, and evaluating references.

You may find your firm's growth constrained by inability to hire good full-time employees because of tight labor markets, emerging technologies, or a dearth of multi-lingual, culturally competent people, for example. Ask yourself whether there are people on the sidelines of the labor markets who can be utilized somehow; some businesses have turned to retirees and maternity-leavers and equipped them to work from home, often on flexible hours, with great success.

Internship programs, properly structured, are excellent recruiting and talent-filtering tools. Adding university or technical school students as interns gives you the benefit of the labor source, but you don't bear all the costs associated with full-time employees. You have an opportunity to evaluate their skills and attitudes without long-term commitment. If appropriate, you can choose to bring them on full-time, but, if necessary, you can scale back your operations by not renewing the intern contracts. In either case, the interns gain valuable work experience and opportunities to network outside their academic community.

Confirm Requirements: If your firm is having difficulty finding qualified candidates for certain positions, reconsider the assumptions underlying the desired qualifications:

- Are the requirements realistic, or would it take a superhero to meet all the "desired qualifications"?

- Is the compensation within industry norms, appropriate to the regional and local economy?

- Is the position advertised effectively, in the right journals, newspapers, association newsletters, or websites?

- Does your firm have a reputation as a good place to work, or are candidates avoiding it because of rumors the company is in trouble financially?

- Are you living up to your own advertising, welcoming candidates, following-up promptly and appropriately after interviews, responding promptly and appropriately to candidate queries?

Example: *One firm had been unable to fill a crucial role after two months of advertising and recruiting: review of the job description showed the requirements were unrealistic. Finding <u>one</u> individual with outstanding technical (IT) skills <u>plus</u> quantitative (mathematical) skills <u>plus</u> highly-developed project management skills <u>plus</u> emotional competencies necessary to lead and manage in a fluid environment was a very tall order.*

A person who could satisfy all those requirements would not have followed any typical career path; if she could be found, her skills would be worth about twice what the company was offering.

Seeking two people, one with outstanding IT and project management skills, and anther with advanced mathematical skills made far more sense. Two people cost more than one, but the more focused approach soon yielded several excellent candidates; the two selected worked very well together.

Pay More, Hire Less: Quality is *always* better than quantity in staff populations: reduce the number of hires, pay each as much as necessary to secure the best talent available. Explain the policy to new hires and current staff retained after performance evaluations: each one is chosen because they have the potential to contribute at gold-standard level. If you have selected the right people, your confidence will inspire and motivate them.

Seek Talent Over Experience: Talented individuals can gain experience on the job, but those with only experience are unlikely to gain talent. If you find two individuals with generally equal technical talent, choose the candidate with the greater emotional intelligence.

If experience among otherwise-qualified employees is a tie-breaker, be certain the experience reported is genuinely apropos: does the individual have twenty years of steadily increasing responsibility, or one year of experience, repeated twenty times?

Everyone Recruits: Ask everyone in the company for their assistance with recommendations to HR and search committees; emphasize the value of their personal and professional networks to the company and their personal knowledge of a potential hire's integrity, diligence, and competence.

Reward Those Who Find Talent: A cash bonus to individuals who recommend someone who is hired and stays at least six months is reasonable. Extra vacation days, gift certificates, or paid travel bonuses acknowledging the contribution are also useful.

Example: A software firm's planned growth was at risk for delay in a very tight labor market; hundreds of thousands of dollars had been spent with external recruiting firms, with little success. Executives adopted a more radical approach: staff members were offered $10,000 for each successful recruiting recommendation.

Recommendation bonuses are a proven recruiting technique: $10,000 is a sufficiently attractive sum to motivate most people; in this case, nearly every person in the company immediately and actively sought recruits, exercising every means at their *disposal, including alumni lists and family connections. The entire company became a highly motivated sales force; excellent candidates were located, recruited and hired.*

Follow Your Own Procedures! Stick to the hiring plans developed in collaboration with HR: taking short-cuts in moments of desperation makes you a value-destroyer.

Example: A European firm struggling to fill some key positions diligently evaluated all their people, necessary roles, studied the market to better understand appropriate compensation levels, wrote a hiring plan and set about advertising their openings, recruiting, and conducting interviews.

The labor market was extremely competitive; few applicants, much less qualified candidates, materialized. After two months of searching, management was desperate and decided to offer a position to one candidate all agreed was not well-qualified.

Worse still, management waived some of the requirements of the hiring plan to expedite the hire; among the requirements waived were reference checks, reference verification and evaluation. The applicant had previously worked in another country, half-way around the world; time zone differences made contacting references difficult anyway, and the pressured atmosphere contributed to the failure of due diligence.

Not surprisingly, the newly hired person did not succeed. The firm was forced to terminate employment and begin the entire process over again, after losing considerable time, desperately needed productivity, and, perhaps, most damaging, some staff confidence.

The moral of the story is simple: hiring plans are devised, and comprehensive evaluations are undertaken, to impose discipline. Ignoring guidelines and protocols precisely when they are most needed is self-defeating. You either believe in your plans and intend to follow them, or you do not.

If you do not believe in your plans, you should have made better ones!

As the leader, you can heavily influence recruitment, but there are cases where you must act with restraint. In particular, do not hire your friends! The only exception is when you know they are good people *and* the *full* interview process is completed *without* your input. When your friends are being considered, the challenge is getting honest feedback from colleagues if they are aware of the relationship: they may be concerned about your reaction in the event they disagree with your choice.

On a much more personal level, when you feel besieged by heavy responsibilities, you may yearn—consciously or subconsciously—for someone familiar and loyal around you; someone you know, can relax with and confide in. Avoid this temptation—it's lonely at the top.

Emotionally competent individuals build their own personal support systems: you must do this proactively by turning to family, friendships unrelated to work, and especially mentors and friends in similar positions in other companies who understand your frustrations—each in turn a sounding-board for others, individuals to whom each turns, assured of confidential, candid advice, counsel, and occasionally, commiseration.

Retention

The exodus of good people is an obvious symptom of a troubled firm; since there is rarely much depth in ailing firms, losing just a few productive individuals leaves significant gaps in the firm's ability to deliver products, manage client relationships, and carry out basic business functions. These gaps must be filled urgently and come with significant recruiting and hiring costs.

Maximizing retention of good people minimizes recruiting-related costs (in terms of time, money, anxiety, and distraction). Lyle Spencer, Jr., of Hay/McBer consulting, estimates the average cost of replacing a mid-level employee is the equivalent of about one year's salary.

Recruiting costs for even junior positions can be in the tens of thousands of dollars; more senior positions can cost several times this figure when using corporate recruiting companies (headhunters).

Spending time and money replacing good people is a shame because it's far more efficient to retain those good people in the first place; however, spending time on replacing poor performers is consistent with your mandate to remove weak links.

Good employees always have more options outside the firm than the less-stellar performers; they are much more likely to be targeted by headhunters and command better compensation packages elsewhere.

Retention efforts are, unfortunately, often reactive: the most intimate discussion held with an employee is the one undertaken *after* the person announces departure from the firm to pursue other interests.

Some relevant questions for exit interviews:

- Where are you heading now?

- What role were you offered?

- What has been missing from your experience here?

- Why are you unhappy here?

- What could this firm have done differently, so we would not be having this conversation?

Answers to exit-interview questions are useful, because you can discern whether losing some employees is a problem, or a symptom of a larger problem. By the time you get to this question-and-answer session it's too late to retain that particular employee. Ending up at an exit interview with a good employee is a failure. The best way to avoid having to ask questions 1 and 2 is by proactively asking your staff questions 3, 4 and 5.

The most common reason for an employee's departure is dislike for a manager. The offender may be a direct manager of the departing person, or a more influential, senior member of the organization.

Any manager at *any* level who is emotionally incompetent and/or ignores the drivers of human behavior discussed earlier in this book is setting the inevitable in motion—driving employees out of the firm.

A departing employee may not have suffered directly at the hands of a bad manager; a junior person, who observes others being repeatedly abused by a senior executive, may conclude there is no future at the firm and elect to leave.

Occasionally, a number of people may leave together to join another entity or set up their own company, usually led by a charismatic and respected leader. Such *en masse* departures can seriously deplete an entire business line or division: avoid critical losses of qualified staff by identifying:

- Competent, charismatic leaders, who command the respect of others;

- Individuals gifted with collaboration and motivation skills, lacking only business experience;

- Disliked or incompetent managers.

Competent leaders, particularly among teams doing work critical to the core business, can make—or break—your company's ability to thrive and prosper: retaining their services, and the employees loyal to them, is a very high priority.

When you identify a disliked manager, immediately consider:

- Removing him from the department;

- Putting him on administrative leave while investigating his performance and the causes for his direct reports' dissatisfaction;

- If he has redeeming qualities, consider reassignment to a new role where his positive attributes are emphasized, or, as a last resort,

- Terminating his employment.

- Consider reassigning victimized employees to a more worthy leader who can help to heal their trauma and re-establish their loyalty to the firm.

Always consider employment termination as a *last resort* for an offending manager with too-few redeeming qualities; be absolutely certain your performance evaluation is correct before terminating anyone!

Investigate present and past complaints thoroughly; very carefully weigh the value of an individual's institutional knowledge and memory against the cost of losing it.

Even disliked managers have the potential for taking much-needed expertise (or staff) with them. If, or when, you do conclude that his negative influence outweighs his current and potential value, terminate his employment quickly and cleanly. A reviled person departing from a position of influence can have an immediate, positive effect on staff.

If, in the first few weeks and months after you join, people continue to depart, do not blame yourself unduly: in most of these cases, the decision to leave came months earlier; your arrival will merely coincide with the end of their negotiations with another firm. Any decision to leave an employer is difficult for most people, and occurs only after significant internal introspection. Once an employee crosses a certain emotional threshold, it's effectively impossible to set the clock back. Realistically—regardless of how much charisma you bring to the table—it's unlikely that you'll reverse a person's decision to leave, especially when the firm's dire condition appears to offer no future.

Some people may choose to leave because they disagree with your philosophy, or because they had hoped to see someone else, possibly a person more familiar to them, in your post. Executives who hoped to be the person filling your post may also leave.

Reach out to people who have decided to leave; debrief them fully to understand why they are leaving, and what it would have taken to retain them. An honest debrief will help you to create a more constructive environment for those who remain. People who know they have an alternative lined up are also much more likely to be open about their reason for departure; take advantage of this willingness to gain important feedback and learn what strongly-held opinions about previous and current management influenced their decision to leave.

Exit interviews are your last, best opportunity for full, honest feedback; if you expect a departing employee won't open up to you (for any reason), identify someone else within the firm *whom you trust* and have him engage in a sufficiently intimate conversation to gather the critical feedback. *"Whom you trust"* requires thoughtful exercise of your intuition and judgment: you don't want to be influenced by anyone else's personal agenda. The person close enough to the departing employee to have an intimate conversation may also, consciously or subconsciously, filter the exit interview information. You need objective observations.

Light the Lamp at the End of the Tunnel: The Mission Statement, Business Plan, and proactive policies are tools you use to sell your vision to lenders and other external stakeholders: use them internally to show those who remain committed during the turnaround their potential earnings. Awarding equity stakes or options, with at least partial vesting in the near-term, may entice the bold risk-takers so necessary to success to stay.

Example: *Consider two firms, both struggling to retain qualified staff.*

Company A management agreed to employee options awards that vested partially over the course of two years (50% vested after one year, 50% vested after two years).

Company B management decided to offer options to select employees with full vesting five years after the award date.

Predictably, the offering from Company A was far more compelling; the firm had much greater success in retention than Company B. Five years for vesting, particularly in a troubled firm, was so far outside the key people's planning horizon the offer added very little weight to the argument for staying. The departures deepened the firm's problems.

Enhance Environments: Space planning and amenities are overlooked, or considered unnecessary expenses, in both distressed and successful firms. Space-planning, attractive and functional décor, natural light and openness attract and welcome employees and clients alike. Effective ventilation, heating and air-conditioning in the space costs less than inefficient units: clean, adequate restrooms and lunchrooms are *not* negotiable.

Example: *One well-known, influential recruiter walks through client facilities and looks for "tells" about management attitude toward employees. Is cardboard taped over vents or air returns? Are there sweaters over the backs of chairs, personal heaters under the desks, or people working in shirt sleeves and fans running on every desk? Are the paper towels and tissues the cheapest brands? Are cubicles and offices all exactly alike, with no personal photos or children's art work displayed? Are people engaged, or merely "looking busy" for the visitor?*

He has been known to turn potential clients down on such observable evidence that the employer really does not consider employee comfort necessary to productivity.

Locate company facilities near excellent day-care facilities; better yet, subsidize those facilities, or sponsor on-site daycare with transportation to and from school for elementary school students. Welcome children to your offices, set aside some space to accommodate them for short periods or special events.

Recognize and Reward Outstanding Contributions: Give credit where it is due. Not all rewards need to be financial. Surveys of employee safety groups showed *no_difference* in safety consciousness and reduced accidents between companies who *recognized* the safest teams with presentation of certificates in small ceremonies, versus companies that funded lavish trips or other expensive rewards for high safety scores.

Example: *A few years ago I ran into a former classmate; the conversation quickly moved to our respective careers. She said she had decided to leave her job, even before finding another; she was so frustrated with her current employer she felt she had to leave, despite liking many of the people and accepting belt-tightening imposed a few months earlier when the firm's performance stalled.*

"You know, I just don't feel appreciated. No one ever acknowledges the hard work I do. If my boss just noticed, congratulated me once in a while, it would be different."

I didn't know her boss; I am not familiar with her company, but I do know my classmate. I believe she would have decided to stay (she resigned a few weeks later) had there been any effort by management to recognize her contributions; no additional financial compensation would have been required. She would have stayed if there had been simple recognition of her contributions, or thanks for a job well done.

I gathered that her boss, who was also the owner, had become very depressed and withdrawn as the firm's performance declined; he was so consumed by concern about the firm that he lost track of the fact that his people were the firm: the firm's fortunes declined as the quality of his interactions with staff declined.

Assist Employees with Retirement Fund Contributions: To the degree possible; match their contributions as revenues allow. Outsource the management of 401K or other retirement funds if staff lack necessary expertise, or in-house management stretches staff too far.

Level the Playing Field: All staff members must have equal opportunities and equal access: give everyone equal time in meetings to express opinions; abolish artificial ceilings. Promote deserving candidates who may have been discriminated against in the past, without fanfare or causing embarrassment to the person in question—the news will sweep through the company, giving hope to others. Perks such as parking, exercise club memberships or access to company facilities should be similar for all staff.

Development and Promotion

Address Individual Competency Actively: Very few individuals are "perfect" for any position: everyone can improve their technical and emotional skills.

Best Practices require strong, carefully crafted policies instructing managers to work closely with direct reports to hone existing skills and learn new ones. Abolish one-time annual reviews in favor of less formal, more continual, two-way feedback.

Sales Managers responsible for training should accompany trainees on as many sales calls as possible to solidify the theory and techniques taught. If the inexperienced salesperson chooses words poorly or pushes for the sale too soon, the manager can ask for a break, suggest a better approach privately, and continue.

Employees who behave abruptly with colleagues, ignore their feedback or behave disrespectfully must be corrected promptly, privately, and firmly. If the behavior is a rare outburst, an apology to the disrespected colleague is probably sufficient; if the employee is a "habitual offender," stronger measures, up to and including probation, Behavior Contracts or other improvement plans, may be necessary. As a final resort, failure to comply could lead to termination.

Upward mobility for staff does not include promoting people prematurely. It may be tempting to fill a more senior role internally; logistically, it's easier; it may appear to be cheaper, but you still must adhere to the principle of putting the right people in the right roles. There is a big difference between being a good individual producer, and a good leader or a good manager.

Premature promotion is bad for all concerned, especially for the person being promoted inappropriately; it is also a symptom of senior management incompetence.

Premature promotion is a symptom of failures in several steps in the recruiting, hiring, evaluating performance and promotion continuum: management's misunderstanding of a person's capabilities, failure to thoroughly evaluate both the business skills and emotional competencies of candidates, failure to recognize knowledge and experience gaps and craft individual development plans.

Mistaking success in technical or customer service spheres as evidence of leadership competence sets up unrealistic expectations for the new manager. His lack of managerial skills will eventually manifest, causing anxiety and stress, ultimately resulting in a loss of self-confidence. Affected staff will also become frustrated and less productive.

Putting a recently-promoted person back into his original role will seem like a career setback, accompanied by embarrassment. Instead of prematurely promoting a person, mentor him, allow him short-term lateral assignments to gain broader experience; when the time comes, he'll have the appropriate skills for a successful transition. Promoting someone prematurely may be the surest way to disrupt his career.

Support Internal and External Development Programs: Tuition assistance and defraying costs of Continuing Education workshops for employees who must retain licenses or credentials are excellent investments.

Setting aside space and time during normal work hours for study, "quiet hours," work with an outside mentor or simply time to think without interruption are invaluable and appreciated.

Introduce New Perspectives: Bring in outside speakers to address industry issues, or present completely different topics of general or inspirational interest. "Brown bag" or informal gatherings where everyone is at ease and can ask questions are particularly effective for buoying morale.

Insisting on industry-specific presentations, with immediate and tangible benefits only, is short-sighted because technical information and expertise is such a small factor in overall performance.

Encourage Intra-Company Movement: Opportunities for temporary or permanent lateral moves to gain new experiences, "internships" for technical staff in other departments, and short-term membership on internal performance-auditing teams are excellent for both morale and productivity.

Any opportunity to learn about and appreciate the challenges others face in their daily work has value; the employees who make the most of their chances to learn and grow are demonstrating their own commitment to the firm.

Set Clear, Achievable Goals for Promotion: Promotion policy must clearly outline requirements in both technical and management tracks, for both technical and emotional competencies.

Managers are responsible for developing their people: those who fail to clearly explain expectations to their direct reports and agree upon advancement plans have, by definition, failed in their responsibility and should not be considered for promotion themselves.

Example: *I was once charged with taking over a successful unit being effectively run by two junior people. One had advanced technical skills; the other complemented those skills with advanced subject-matter expertise and well-developed emotional competencies, which proved highly effective in winning the trust of clients.*

One of my first tasks was to review their performance and set a timeline for promotion, which would follow once they attained competence in agreed-upon skills. I suggested a plan I thought was fair and proactive.

To my initial surprise, each displayed obvious dissatisfaction. Delving a little deeper into their concerns, each one opened up and pointed out (in separate conversa-

tions) that they had been given similar plans in the past, completed review periods successfully by the standards given, only to be told that new promotion guidelines had been adopted and their skills still fell short.

My greatest surprise was that the two were still there! I certainly could not blame them for their skepticism concerning my plan, especially when they had been burned multiple times in the past. Winning their trust required all my emotional competence and negotiating skills.

I struck agreements with company executives guaranteeing promotion for both, if and when I concluded they met the necessary skill thresholds and revenue targets, also certified by senior management. The contracts between my staff and me, and senior management and me, transparently documented and cemented the new goals. When each one met the agreed-upon requirements, I personally championed their cases to senior management, again, securing their promotions.

The message: agree on the goals, and honor your word.

Employment Termination

Relieving an individual of the means to earning his livelihood is a very great responsibility, never to be taken lightly, and the last resort.

Human Resources professionals represent the firm and its interests—not the employees'. Every employee must understand this fact of employment life, from their first orientation forward; it allows them to seek personal guidance, legal counsel or union support should the employee deem it advisable.

Many managers find delivering a termination notice the most difficult aspect of their jobs.

Example: *Early in my managerial career I had to terminate the employment of a person who'd been with the company for many years. I agonized over the decision for weeks, especially during the week leading to the actual dismissal.*

With the benefit of hindsight, I realized that what I dreaded most was delivering the message—not the logic of the decision itself. The person in question was a low-producer who also stifled the productivity of others. There was no question in my mind about that. What I dreaded was looking him in the eye and saying the words that would affect his livelihood, family, and self-esteem.

Fortunately, I was accompanied by a highly experienced HR staffer who supported me through the process. This helped a lot, but didn't completely shield me from anxiety.

Take Action Professionally and Promptly: Performance evaluations are the basis of every employment decision: if an employee simply does not have the requisite skills, is unwilling or unable to learn them, or retraining is not practical, recognize and accept the facts. Most employees in that situation find termination a relief from the stress of knowing they're not performing adequately.

If an employee has behaved in any way that requires terminating employment "for cause," swift action is absolutely necessary.

Example: *I recently had an opportunity to share my experiences with a young manager who was having extreme difficulty with an employee who was clearly disrespectful and disruptive. The employee undermined the manager's authority, used foul language, and refused to co-operate with colleagues.*

The young manager was conflicted. On the one hand, he observed his authority being undermined publicly, causing embarrassment to himself and damaging the productivity of his entire team. On the other, he was concerned that complaining about the employee was a reflection of his failure as a leader.

After watching the young manager putting himself, and the employee, through a few very tough days of giving second, third, and fourth chances, I stepped in and reviewed the sequence of events of the past few weeks. I established with him, logically, that there was no alternative but to terminate employment, and that we, as management, had an obligation to the entire office to do so. I offered to assist him in delivering this message, and was impressed to hear that, although he was clearly anxious, he felt it was his obligation to lead the conversation without me.

In contrast to my first employment termination experience, I personally felt no remorse about this one. I knew the right decision was being made to protect other employees.

Expecting an employee being dismissed "for cause" to "go quietly" is unrealistic: policy requiring an HR professional to be present at all termination interviews is highly recommended. Termination interviews should be formally scheduled, follow established protocols, with conversations and events documented thoroughly and accurately.

The employee from the example above was true to form: he began to shout and threaten the manager. Fortunately, his behavior was anticipated: he was escorted out of the building, off company property, by security staff standing by at the HR professional's request.

Provide Placement Assistance: Some firms put outplacement specialists on staff when closing plants or offices is necessary. Others contract with outplacement firms.

The degree of assistance paid for should reflect the reason for terminating employment: large-scale layoffs or letting go employees who simply cannot keep up with changing technology is very different from an employee who has harassed colleagues and refused to desist, or one who has committed fraud against the company.

Formulate Equitable Severance Packages: If you are terminating employment without notice, but *not* for cause, allow the employee(s) sufficient salary to pay basic living expenses while searching for another position, along with legally-required/any accumulated retirement, vacation or sick leave pay, and continue to pay insurance premiums for a reasonable period. Support the employee's right to unemployment benefits.

When terminating employment for cause, such as fraud, workplace violence, or failing to comply with a probation agreement, use state and local laws as your policy guidelines. Rewarding a person who refuses to cease harassment or other harmful behavior with a "golden parachute" violates common sense and is disrespectful of his victims and colleagues.

Seek Amicable Separations: Avoid internal or external recriminations: even when an employee is being fired for cause, confidentiality is still a legal right.

Consider the reasons for terminating employment when faced with a less-than-clear cut situation. An employee who simply lacks sufficient emotional intelligence to learn to behave appropriately at work may be seen differently by your state's employment laws than one who is intellectually limited (a member of a protected class).

Employees who have been warned, reprimanded, and agreed to Behavioral Contracts which they then refuse to abide by, are also entitled to protection under the law.

When faced with unclear situations, get very good legal advice, and consider a financial settlement with the individual that precludes a lawsuit for wrongful termination and requires that settlement sums and conditions remain strictly confidential, preferably with a written contract stating the consequences for breaking confidences.

Terminating the employment of poorly-performing managers or executives must follow the same protocol:

- Observe and evaluate performance according to consistent, transparent, legal, ethical, fair rules;

- Investigate complaints promptly, objectively, and thoroughly;

- Follow policy and procedure for corrective actions to the letter, documenting agreements completely;

- Schedule the final appointment to allow the executive to have an advisor present, if he so chooses;

- Maintain the strictest confidence for all parties concerned; reach confidentiality agreements regarding any settlement.

Finally, when a highly-visible senior executive's employment is terminated, or negative publicity surrounds an employee accused of fraud against the company or other criminal actions, prepare the appropriate public statements in advance, coach other executives who may be waylaid unexpectedly by reporters or others seeking a statement, and let the professional HR and/or public relations staff handle the rest.

Avoid Firing Cycles: "Seeking a savior" is a fairly common reaction when companies are troubled: this quarter, Management Philosophy A holds sway; five years later, it's Management Philosophy Z.

Example: *Team A comes in, assesses and evaluates, and decides to let a few people go, but the company is still unhealthy. Team B, Team C, Team D come in over a period of a few years, and repeat the process, according to their particular lights, and the cycle of winnowing the remaining talent to find the right combination continues.*

Some Board members and senior executives charged with appointing and hiring the new management teams might excuse this extremely expensive, wasteful, and demoralizing process as "markets in action" or describe it as "preparing for the future" or some other nonsense, rather than admit they are failing to recognize and honor their human assets as their most valuable capital assets.

Firing cycles are a clear symptom of the deeper problem: the company leadership is failing, because they do not fully understand their business in terms of their markets, competition, and macroeconomic factors, and/or because they lack sufficient emotional competence to lead and manage effectively.

Emotionally incompetent leaders are most likely to miss the most important point of this discussion: the professional and personal consequences to employees mirror the ultimate consequences for the company as a whole—particularly the leaders making the poor choices that bring disgrace upon themselves for failing their investors.

CHAPTER 9
Turn Your Company Around

In the previous chapter, setting the necessary people-related actions in motion was discussed.

This chapter lays out how to implement technical and process-related changes in concert with people-related actions; specifically, setting a constructive corporate culture, putting in place solid internal processes, revising offerings, and mending or improving partner and client relationships build on previous chapters.

Corporate Culture

Historically, "culture"—the sum of a group's beliefs, ways of thinking, behaving, reacting and teaching others to behave—was associated almost exclusively with nationality or ethnicity. Certain nationalities were assumed to possess an abundance of one skill or another, and were closely identified with that "gift." Many of these were stereotypes, some quite offensive.

Do not mislabel people or organizations based on nationality, race, or ethnicity; you must not allow any of your staff to harbor such unfounded, blanket opinions.

The point bears repeating: do not allow prejudices or biases based on attitudes toward race, nationality, or ethnicity to influence *any* behavior in the workplace or corporate decisions.

Globalization and diverse labor forces have intensified the frequency and duration of our experiences with people from other cultures, and, fortunately, opened many eyes to the delights and benefits of diversity.

In England, a very diverse nation, a typical small firm is likely to employ individuals with at least half-a-dozen different nationalities; large firms commonly have several dozen such groups; multinationals may have over one hundred groups represented. Culture is becoming less synonymous with nationality and increasingly summarized by some subset of descriptors from the (partial) list below:

- Youthful or old-fashioned;

- Comfortable, or uncomfortable, with new technology;

- Informal or formal;

- Hierarchical or non-hierarchical;

- Internally or externally focused;

- Committed to promote from within, or inclined to hire managers from outside the firm;

- Academic or non-academic;

- Quantitative or qualitative;

- Penny-pinching or generous;

- Open to ideas or closed to them.

As far as influencing the performance of any business unit, cultures can be constructive, destructive, or neutral. Strive to advance cultural traits that can help to build positive momentum; that is, those that provide comparative advantages.

Work to remove or mitigate destructive cultural influences in a parallel function: in a troubled company, it's even more likely that certain cultural traits are contributing to dysfunction.

A single, uniform culture shared by all is essential to cohesive effort, the bedrock for any success at all in following a Mission Statement.

A culture that values excellence and collaboration, rewards those who embrace these values and measures progress in those terms, underlies every successful Business Plan.

Given the fast-paced changes in technology, a culture that can comfortably embrace technological changes is a competitive advantage: inclusiveness and openness allow everyone to contribute—a necessity for a resource-constrained turnaround candidate.

Not wasting time on ceremony breaks down too-rigid territorial and other conventional barriers to "cross pollination" of ideas, bringing new groups into contact for dynamic new combinations of complementary skills and insights.

Independence and resourcefulness guided and directed by the Mission Statement, tolerance for failure/willingness to entrust resources to bold, creative solutions, are hallmarks of successful companies.

Satisfying individual and collective yearning for transparency and mutual respect is the ultimate goal for all diverse cultures.

As you work toward a unified culture, however, note that uniformity can potentially lead to narrowness of vision, clearly an eventuality to avoid. Consider the accessibility of your existing, or intended, cultures. A very academic culture may be a difficult place for a non-academically inclined person to find a home. Think about what you want your culture to emphasize, and why those traits and values are desirable, useful, and the likelihood of them causing unintended harm to individuals or the company as a whole.

Making changes in an organization's culture can be a very difficult undertaking: culture, whether corporate or community, can be a very powerful identifier for people. Accordingly, it's advisable to re-orient existing culture subtly, rather than attempting to confront it head-on with the intention of drastically changing it. By choosing the latter, you are very likely to rock the institution to its very foundations. A predictable outcome may be mass departures by people who so strongly identify with their culture that they don't feel they can handle work in a different environment.

Do not make drastic changes to cultures you don't yet understand. Even if things rub you the wrong way, recognize that you are seeing *them* through the filter of *your* own biases and prejudices; make sure you understand the patterns of the fabric that holds people together before forcing change upon them. Tearing this fabric can, and will, cause at least some disruption and strife.

Example: Early in my managerial career, I encountered a good example of cultural differences when I was assigned to manage a team with people based in both New York and London. The New York culture was relatively relaxed about hierarchies. It was clearly understood who managed whom, but there was no ceremonial pretense around the reporting structure. A cross section of associates, managers, and managing directors could and did go out for a drink, and mingled comfortably. In contrast, the London office was more aware of hierarchies.

I had small teams in each location and significant recruiting needs in both. I was facing the typical challenge for small units or firms—no one had the time to do the recruiting and interviewing. The mid-level and senior-level managers were so stretched, working with clients, they found it very difficult to find the time for anything else.

I set out to devise an efficient way to fill our staffing gaps without disrupting the teams, and came up with the idea of involving junior staff members in interviewing potential peers or candidates for more senior roles.

I liked the idea for several reasons: we would have more people available to examine incoming candidates. There would be less pressure on our senior staff, who could not physically interview everyone. We could also avoid a situation in which a mid-level manager was interviewed only by senior people, hired, and then discovered to have a significant personality clash with the junior staff. Finally, involving junior staff members would send a message of inclusiveness, making it clear that their opinions were valued, and they were not viewed as mindless or nameless "cheap labor."

We began in New York, involving everyone we could in recruiting. Occasionally, junior personnel were called upon to interview mid-level managers—people who could potentially be their bosses. This worked well. One junior staffer had been a military officer before turning to business; his maturity and alertness were quite effective, and he had all the right instincts in sizing people up. I was quite pleased with the results and (silently) declared victory.

Then I attempted to extend this idea to the London team. I had even higher hopes for the London-based team, because I knew there had historically been issues with junior staff members disliking their managers. In fairness, the managers had not behaved very well. I anticipated a warm reception to this egalitarian idea, which would give assurances to the junior staff that no nasty new managers would be installed in place of the departing ones.

To my great surprise, my announcement that we would proceed with this approach was met with much concern by the junior staff.

Following several one-on-one discussions, it became clear that there were two sets of responses. One group felt comfortable, while the other was utterly horrified by the idea. Perhaps predictably, with the benefit of hindsight, the former response came from people of more liberal cultures, and the latter from more strict ones. In the interest of fairness and consistency, I decided not to involve any of the junior staffers in recruiting for the London office, and instead spent more time there myself, interviewing each and every candidate.

While time-consuming, I personally found this to be so useful that I have since been involved with almost every hire made into my teams, at any level.

The more important lesson for me, of course, was the realization that a solution that works well in one culture may well be a disaster in another.

The only time head-on, confrontational changes might be considered appropriate is when the culture is one that supports corruption, dishonesty, fraud or other illegal behavior. Removing the ring leaders and their supporters is usually sufficient—and quite often a relief to the rest of the employees, fearful of retribution from the corrupt few.

When an incumbent culture is so devastating to the firm's progress that it does require very drastic measures, including an overt head-on collision to dismantle racist or sexist cliques, be aware of the enormity of the effect before you take action, and be certain you are prepared to manage the aftershocks.

Internal Processes and Controls

Any successful turnaround relies heavily on improving, replacing or adding new processes; we discussed assessing existing processes in an earlier chapter. It is now time to address action items. Clearly, the processes and controls you must put in place will be specific to your situation; this section stresses high-level improvements/replacements for existing processes. You must tailor these to fit your firm's specific needs.

Some Common Processes

As a starting point, consider the processes reviewed in Chapter 4, which included Client Relationship Management, Billing, Contracting, Human Resources, Payroll, and Time Tracking.

Each of these processes rests, to greater and lesser degrees, on Information Technology. IT systems are the greatest bane and blessings of modern companies; correctly structured and used, IT systems protect against a host of internal and external risks by bringing data together in sufficiently-compact and detailed formats for meaningful analysis.

Back Up the Back Up: Priority One is preserving critical data, whether it regards clients, operations, accounting, finance, marketing, legal, email, documenting intellectual property, or who comes in and out the front and back doors.

Preserving Critical Data: In addition to providing adequate space for staff, hardware, and software, includes:

- Redundant controls for physical risks:

    A. Access to facilities by unauthorized personnel, disgruntled employees, criminals or others bent on property damage;

    B. Excessive temperature fluctuations caused by equipment or power failures;

    C. Fire, flood, earthquake or other natural disasters, and the subsequent power failures;

    D. Power failures caused by malfunctions in the grid, whether by accident, equipment failure, or terrorists.

- Redundant controls for human risks:

    A. Monitoring systems to prevent, track and identify attempts to disable, hack, invade, or compromise programs or data;

B. Strict protocols for authorizing individual access to data, particularly mission-critical and proprietary files;

C. Control of laptop and other portable means of access to *any* company data;

D. Protocols for records that may be downloaded, even temporarily, on laptops, etc.;

E. Strict controls on employee access to the Internet; computers used for necessary market or technical research, access to on-line journals, etc., are (ideally) separate from the critical data systems.

- Secure, off-site transport and storage:

A. Even very small companies need off-site storage for critical electronic records; using a bonded storage facility for long-term records storage is an excellent option;

B. Larger companies with adequate resources can build their own record depositories to specifications designed to minimize both physical and human risks.

- Staged transport of records—end-of-shift or daily backups can be maintained on premises or transported by bonded companies to near-by bank vaults, etc.; accumulated, or longer-term backups, can be transported from the vault to the bonded storage facility, etc.

Any leader, executive, manager, supervisor, or data entry clerk who leaves IT security to chance or violates security protocols poses an unacceptable risk.

Follow the Business Plan: Technology changes frequently, but the iterations are predictable within fairly reasonable margins; the Business Plan should lay out current, short-term, and long-term requirements for hardware and software capacity. Budgets for designing or specifying, acquiring, phasing out and replacing hardware and software may require adjustment from time to time, as will any other expense subject to forecasting; the object is to anticipate accurately, to prevent being hamstrung at critical intersections by uncertainty.

Cut Your Losses: Some systems are so troublesome and expensive to maintain they should simply be taken offline, and never accessed again.

Choose the Right People: Many profess to be IT specialists, but not all are created equal.

Many IT certification program graduates are excellent technicians, well qualified in their specialty, but no academic certification guarantees —cannot measure, for that matter—a graduate's practical knowledge, skills, productivity, intellectual or emotional competence, or their professionalism.

Develop Specifications: Compiling and documenting all the necessary features needed from a particular IT (software or hardware) product requires input from all parties concerned, careful evaluation, and considerable investment in time and expertise.

Setting correct priorities is as integral to IT specifications as any other Business Plan component: agreement with the head of IT and her staff regarding which solutions are most mission-critical is the first step.

Look at the staff you have, their expertise and experience; work with finance and other relevant stakeholders to decide whether to build internally or purchase a solution that meets the most immediate and critical needs.

Example: A company's Chief Technical Officer (CTO) urged the head of a division's IT department to complete a full characterization of requirements for a Customer Relations Management (CRM) system.

The analysis yielded a list of all the features required to meet the division's needs as it dealt with clients and prospects globally, from its sales force to its product management to its billing department. The team was organized, precise, and attentive to the needs of all business units.

Specifications in hand, the division IT department head briefed the CTO and was given approval to acquire. After a careful search, several providers were identified. The IT team proceeded with a proof-of-concept from all short-listed vendors and selected one that provided an extremely good fit with the documented specifications and was able to prove that its software product existed, functioned well, and was in use by several other customers. References confirmed the customers were very happy.

A month after the contract was signed, the implementation was in full swing. The division IT department head then received a call from the CTO—who advised that a corporate-level decision had been made to go with a different CRM product across the entire firm.

Incredulous, and mightily embarrassed, the division IT department head had to approach the vendor team working in the office, apologize, and ask them to leave.

Later that day, the CTO grumpily explained that he'd been outvoted in a Board meeting; a single solution across the entire global corporation was chosen, viewed as a way to increase economies of scale and reduce maintenance costs. The CTO apologized, admitting that consideration of this high-level decision had not been divulged.

The new system met less than half the division's requirements: salespeople and the billing department had to maintain portions of client records outside the system, creating a manual, incomplete, time-consuming parallel process.

Adding insult to injury, bookkeepers at company headquarters would periodically call to complain about errors and inconsistencies in the division's customer records.

Many observations and lessons can be drawn from this example.

First, it was unforgivable to allow the IT head to complete such a detailed investigation without revealing the internal deliberations about a completely different system.

Second, many business units, divisions, and entire global corporations end up with IT solutions that don't meet their needs.

Third, immense efficiency losses and large numbers of frustrated (and less productive) employees result from these poor outcomes.

Outsource: If your firm is not an IT specialist, outsourcing is an excellent option; even for IT firms, outsourcing some operational and support functions allows clearer focus on their own core business.

If you do outsource, insist on a proof-of-concept—a live demonstration, preferably with your data, on your premises, of the tool's functionality—before committing to a vendor.

Many vendors will offer some "works-in-progress" solutions, promising the tools will be "complete" and "seamless" by the time implementation begins on your premises. It's always risky to assume that a work-in-progress will become a successful implementation.

One of the few situations when "works-in-progress" are acceptable is when you seek a highly specialized solution, and your research has convinced you it doesn't exist anywhere else in the world: then, a co-development scheme might make sense. However, since you are essentially the first beta tester for the vendor's newest product, special pricing and support concessions are in order.

Beware of "vaporware," the name whispered for non-existent software, offered in a desperate attempt to gain your business, in the hope that once the contract is signed, the vendor will somehow, miraculously, figure out a way to deliver it.

Example: Employees in a well-known software company in New York used to joke (darkly) when their email and other IT processes broke down constantly, despite the firm having dozens of highly-skilled computer scientists on hand.

The malfunctions reflected management priorities: the best and most creative people—the highly-prized Ph.D.s—were assigned to the firm's crown jewels: developing and testing their own software products for sale to clients. The IT department was, unfortunately, staffed by people considered outsiders by the rest of the firm.

After several years of this unfortunate disconnect, all operational functions were outsourced to another firm.

Bring in Consultants: Contrary to consultant firms' marketing efforts, consultants are not the solution to every problem. However, judicious use of specialists (preferably with no dependencies on vendors) to examine existing systems and give recommendations can be very useful.

There are consultants who can examine the computer code utilized for internal systems and judge their efficacy; sometimes IT problems are due to flaws in the original code base. Some problems can only be identified during code-level analysis, because other applications have been built on top of the original code, obscuring the true source of the failure.

Plan Support and Maintenance: IT systems require ongoing support or maintenance, like any other equipment. Whether you build internally or purchase systems from external sources, put support packages that meet your firm's needs in place as part of the original project.

You may, for example, determine that 24/7 support for your staff or clients is necessary, or 8 a.m. to 5 p.m., 5 days a week is sufficient.

Consider the system users when stating support requirements: degrees of computer literacy vary widely in even small firms.

Important Process Characteristics

Useful processes enhance or enable productivity, seamlessness, reliability, transparency, and scalability.

Productivity: Efficient, effective production is a root problem for troubled companies. Productivity gains—doing more with less—can quickly catapult a firm to greater efficiency and improved health. Gains may arise from training people to do their work more proficiently (accomplishing the same tasks more adeptly), or getting them to do different work (identifying and focusing on meaningful tasks).

Seamlessness: When people and processes blend into the day-to-day, they are "seamless." When people or roles stick out like sore thumbs, constantly upsetting the rhythm of work, they are getting in the way. You must strive to remove bottlenecks from your systems. Besides operational benefits, seamlessness can be a morale booster for staff, who will view a smoothly operating process with great pride.

Reliability: If an operating process is unreliable, it's not really *operating*. This may seem to be an obvious statement, but it must be emphasized that you should embrace robust systems you can depend on. Put good people on the system design, and, if you are turning to outside help, make sure you know what you want, and the supplier you have chosen can be relied upon to deliver a solid system configured to your needs. Improved reliability will also help to regain the confidence of staff, clients, and suppliers.

Transparency: Transparency is necessary if observers are to be comfortable with new processes, and obviates the need to intrude and disrupt operations as they seek (difficult to find) answers. Transparency is necessary for those doing the work to identify ways to improve their processes. Finally, transparency leads to greater accountability, because it's easier to associate individuals with particular responsibilities. When people know they will be held responsible, they tend to have a greater sense of urgency; they tend to work faster and more accurately. The bright light of transparency enhances the quality of information available to you and supports better decision-making. Inept or lazy people who have basked in the dim light of opacity may choose to leave or reform, both positive outcomes for any firm.

Scalability: Your objective as the manager of a turnaround candidate is to achieve positive growth. A natural consequence of growth is that additional capacity is required to support the expansion. In the ideal case, the processes you put in place will allow scaling upward, comfortably accommodating the growth. As you build or purchase processes, plan for that growth by selecting flexible and scalable systems. Failure to do so may cause disruptions to your positive momentum.

An important challenge will be to balance accommodating expected future growth against the risk of overcapacity. You don't want to tie up scarce capital in large-scale systems in the expectation of growth, only to realize growth is coming much slower than originally anticipated.

Controls

A critical aspect of processes is that they must be accompanied by appropriate controls. Controls begin with policy statements, which must in turn be consistent with Mission Statements and Business Plans. Controls should include:

- Proper documentation;

- Requiring multiple signatures or sets of eyes;

- Restricting access to sensitive information;

- Unannounced reviews and inspections;

- Periodic personnel reassignments;

- Independent validations of procedures;

- Competitive salaries.

Controls maintain the discipline of processes, enabling them to function as intended. Controls also help to thwart internal and external fraud.

Process Outsourcing

The inevitable need to add processes or re-engineer existing ones creates a temptation to outsource. Sometimes this is the correct answer. But, in other, cases it's not. Consider the following typical sequence of events:

- External consultants come in and spend months getting up to speed on your business. During that period, your people are distracted from their other activities in order to interface with the visiting team and educate its members on your firm's inner workings.

- The visitors then spend time, often months, creating a solution. Again, this involves much of your staff's time, as they work in parallel with the consultants.

- Months or years are spent implementing the solution, with great effort expended by all parties.

- There are then two options:

  A. The external consultants exit the scene and leave you entirely on your own, or

  B. The external consultants leave behind some of their own experts to hold your hand.

You pay good hard cash throughout the process; you also pay in the opportunity cost of your people's time as they are distracted from their daily duties. There are several other liabilities to this approach.

In A, all the expertise is lost once the consultants depart, and the next time you are confronted by a similar challenge, you must again turn to the outside consultants for help, and suffer similar costs and distractions.

In B, the expertise remains in-house, but you don't own it. Instead, you effectively rent it, again at a hefty cost.

While it may be the case that your staff lacks process re-engineering skills initially, don't jump to the conclusion that an external consultant knows more than you do about your business. Developing process re-engineering skills internally means they are thereafter available quickly and cost-efficiently for further work—a significant long-term dividend.

On the other hand, this may well mean a need to invest in resources (new staff) and training, and you will need capable leaders to do the job properly. You must weigh the costs and gains of doing this against your other priorities.

Partners

It's assumed that you've already thoroughly assessed your partners' capabilities, contributions, and deficiencies.

The first important decision is whether each relationship is worth pursuing.

Negotiate New Terms: In some cases, the partnership may be salvageable; but, that may hinge on the willingness of the partner to make important changes: committing more people to the collaboration, living up to their share of responsibilities, making up for past infractions. Revisit the terms of your agreement, renegotiate as necessary, including penalties for non-performance, to ensure expectations are clearly understood and agreed.

Terminate Agreements: Whenever agreements damage your company's prospects, or the partner is not willing to live up to an existing agreement, or re-negotiate in good faith, it's time to go your separate ways. Do so openly and respectfully, explaining why there is insufficient commercial reason to continue.

Example: *I once witnessed an evolving partnership between two firms.*

The first was a very large and reputable company which entered into a joint marketing agreement in support of the second, much smaller partner's flagship (and only) product.

Happy to have the large partner and its global reputation, the small firm agreed to very onerous terms. It accepted that 30% of all revenues for its product would be shared with the large partner, even when the large partner did not actively participate in the sale.

Several years later, the smaller firm had grown significantly, and introduced several new products. When the small firm's marketing director left, his replacement took a close look at the original joint marketing agreement and realized, to his horror, that not only was his company in breach of the contract, it owed the larger firm millions of dollars!

When the deal was originally struck, the small firm's owners had been so desperate to partner with the larger firm, they accepted a clause which allowed the larger firm to lay claim to 30% of all revenues generated by any new product the small firm launched.

Further, there was no time limit on these claims: the larger firm could claim all these revenue streams until the end of time.

The large firm had not closed one single product sale on behalf of the smaller partner since the date of the agreement. In fairness, the larger firm's sales personnel talked to prospects about the partner's products, and they were mentioned in marketing literature, but the larger firm had not contributed meaningfully to a single sale.

In strictly legal terms, the larger firm had met its obligations under the contract; nevertheless, recognizing the potential effect on its future prospects, the small firm's management approached their counterparts in the larger firm, seeking a fair resolution. And they got one! Fortunately, the people they dealt with lived up to their firm's reputation for fairness, recognizing that the agreement really was very unfair; a single payment of several hundred thousand dollars in compensation for formal termination of the marketing agreement resolved the issue.

Seek Better Partners: Some relationships remain in place for years, often purely due to inertia. These agreements are a waste of everyone's time and energy; in a competitive market, there is usually at least one other entity that really needs your firm as a partner. *Find that firm or firm(s)!*

Lead your staff through brainstorming sessions to identify the types of firms that may be a good match for your needs; authorize staff members to search actively for better partners, based on the parameters set during brainstorming.

Think Globally: Good partners may be next door, or on the other side of the world. Authorize distant colleagues to actively seek potential partners for local or distant collaborations, or do it yourself if others are not available or capable.

Example: *An entrepreneurial Asian firm with limited resources came up with an idea for a high-tech system with practical applications in airport and port security.*

They discussed ideas with local engineering and defense firms for eighteen months but made little progress; finally, one of the firm's managing partners decided to seek opportunities elsewhere. He approached one large European engineering firm and was asked to present the ideas to the firm's Board. After an hour, the Board asked him to wait outside: ten minutes later, he was asked to return, and told that they were seeking growth opportunities and were willing to invest several million dollars, so long as they could have the exclusive contract for building the final solutions. They didn't even ask for equity in the entrepreneurial firm!

True to their word, a prototype was built and tested at their facilities.

Several years later, the two sides agreed to even more investment, this time in exchange for an equity stake; the European partner put their global marketing infrastructure to work, to the benefit of all concerned.

The golden opportunity was the result of boldness and confidence, seeking a partner beyond the local region.

Clients

In an earlier section, I urged you to thoroughly assess each client's needs and opinions of your firm as a solution provider. The more comprehensive your initial assessment efforts, the more meaningful your conclusions can be regarding client needs and what you must do to serve those needs. Embrace these conclusions and refine your Value Propositions to make your sales efforts more effective.

Employees distracted by company problems tend to neglect client relationships; some employees may depart, taking with them intimate knowledge of particular clients, and often leave a gaping hole in the relationship. The troubled firm's connection with its clients deteriorates, creating discontinuities, and destroying trust so critical to doing business smoothly. Predictably, clients who are thus affected will seek more meaningful and responsive relationships elsewhere.

Troubled firms may attempt to hide their internal difficulties from clients; inevitably, clients begin to realize that not all is well. Upon your arrival, it's critical to reassure clients that times are changing and their concerns will be dealt with in a timely fashion. Use your judgment to decide what to reveal. In many cases you, as the new leader, may be the best person to deliver that message directly to an important client, rather than a more junior employee. The client will look to you closely for some guarantee that your firm will deliver high quality service or product in uninterrupted fashion. The more honest and transparent you are and the more believable your plans for the future, the more likely you are to gain or retain a client. This is one of those situations where you must choose your words carefully as you tiptoe through a proverbial minefield. It's often after such meetings that you will feel that you've really earned your paycheck.

There are two general types of clients: those with whom you do routine business, and those with whom you have an especially close relationship. The special clients willing to serve as references for your products and/or services are strategically important; it is worthwhile to provide extra service to keep them happy. Striving to provide great service to all clients is necessary to be competitive; however, identifying a handful of well-selected clients and non-clients for their strategic value and making appropriate gestures (discounts, free services) to establish mutually beneficial relationships is essential to the turnaround.

Strategic or reference clients are critical, but not every client can be a reference client. Do not allow your sales staff to claim that everyone is strategically important or risk a deadly cycle of bending over backward, lowering your prices for everyone. The danger of becoming known within the marketplace as a discounter is that counterparties in every negotiation will automatically expect that if they bargain hard, you will lower prices, substantially undermining your pricing strategy.

Improve communication with clients to reduce uncertainties and anxieties the client may have, get a better sense of how you have failed (or may be on the brink of failing) and direct your attention to areas in which you need to manage expectations better.

If you conclude that you have let any client down, offering some benefits, subsidies, or discounts to make up for past wrongs demonstrates remorse and your ongoing commitment.

Consider setting up SLAs clarifying your responsibilities and the client's, outlining conflict or disagreement resolution procedures, and penalties for contract violations, such as reducing the price of your service or deliverable and including additional services or remedial action at no additional cost rather than renegotiate the contract completely. Doing this clearly demonstrates to the client that you are committed to service. It also sends an internal signal that you intend to deliver high quality products or services.

The customer may always be right, but it can be right sometimes to choose not to have that customer. There is such a thing as a bad customer: often, one or a handful of customers will account for the bulk of a firm's maintenance and support costs. In some cases clients may cause problems by treating your staff abusively or behaving dishonestly; you may lose employees who are tired of being subjected to abuse. Bad clients can cost the firm money, efficiency, and personnel; sinking scarce resources into an impossible-to-please client, when those same resources could be more profitably directed to winning and pleasing new clients is ineffective management.

Example: *In the software business, it's most efficient to discontinue old products to avoid the costs of maintaining multiple versions. Some clients insist on using old versions of your products and resist all your efforts to upgrade them to a newer system, thwarting your efforts to decommission old products and platforms that are no longer profitable or efficient. You can sometimes deal with this by charging for extra support, or by providing clients with incentives to upgrade by waiving or reducing upgrade fees. As a rule, you should include contract language allowing you to discontinue certain products or revisit all contract details after a certain number of years or on some schedule triggered by release of new versions of products.*

When you identify bad clients, your first effort should always be to try to resolve the issue in direct dialog. Sometimes, a bilateral solution proves impossible, requiring unilateral action. Inform the client that your company will not renew the contract and seek as quick a separation as possible, acting within the letter of the law and your contract. You may be amazed at the effect this will have on your staff's morale, and the time freed up to engage in more productive activities.

Separation from the client should be a last resort: you are in business to do business, and have, in principle, decided not to do business, risking ramifications and repercussions. The abandoned client may continue to, or begin to, disparage your company publicly, or initiate legal action. Depending on the client institution's standing in the local or global community, negative comments can affect your company's ability to do business with others. Predictably, your competitors will take advantage of damage to your reputation.

Strive for an amicable separation by offering the client something of value in return for a signed agreement in which they give up the option to take legal action, and all parties agree to refrain from making any negative comments about each other. You may need to be creative; consider a version of the software firm example (previous page), in which you give the client the legal right to maintain and update the old software code. The client becomes more self-sufficient, no longer relying on your company for support, retaining a preferred system and the right to alter it in future. Contract language restricting the client's ability to sell the product to anyone else, especially a competitor, would be reasonable and prudent.

CHAPTER 10
Overcome Inevitable Setbacks

Nothing in the world of business ever goes precisely as planned; by definition, you can't prepare fully for surprises, because there's no way to know precisely how and when they'll manifest. The best preparation is to recognize early on that there will be setbacks, and to refuse to allow such momentary disappointments to determine the fate of the enterprise.

In all likelihood, just as you feel some momentum has finally been generated, something will happen to foil your efforts. You'll feel that you've taken one step forward, only to suddenly take two steps back.

Some examples of backward steps include:

- An important product initiative flops.

- Your protégé or a key person leaves: worst case, he goes to the competition.

- An accidental death, serious illness, or some other personal tragedy befalls one or more of the staff.

- A key client defects to the competition.

- An act of war reverses all the gains you've made in a new territory.

- An act of nature destroys your infrastructure and renders you unable to deliver products or support clients.

At the risk of being overly philosophical, the world is an uncertain place; setbacks are suffered daily, by all firms, including healthy ones. There are always unforeseen circumstances. That is the very nature of business. There will be setbacks—count on it! Your objective must be to minimize:

- The frequency of their occurrence, and

- Their severity when they do occur.

Two perspectives must be dealt with when these disruptive events occur. One is your personal perspective; the other is everyone else's.

As the leader, your perspective must remain on the bigger picture. Presumably, you have been given this position because you have exhibited this ability. Your poise, confidence, and cheerleading capacity will be tested. That is precisely what you are being paid for. It's easy to celebrate victories and enjoy fat bonuses when all is going well. Leadership is tested when times are bad; when events go against you. Be visible, be philosophical, and be optimistic.

From the perspective of the staff, these events may be seen very differently. Junior people may be more devastated by a setback than their more mature counterparts, simply because they lack the experience to gauge the relative seriousness of the event and long-term implications.

On an emotional level, people who are thwarted while attempting to make a comeback may be significantly discouraged, particularly those with a predisposition to feelings of inferiority, common in a company that has already suffered humiliations, defeat and dysfunction in the past.

Susceptible people need to be made to understand that losing a battle doesn't mean losing the campaign: they need to see that you and the management team are not devastated by the news. Explain that you do care about losses, but recognize that setbacks are inevitable, and you are committed to victory, and are unflinching in the face of new barriers to success. Set future expectations by emphasizing that such setbacks have happened in the past and will occur in future.

Highlighting lessons learned is critical. Learning and growing from a setback is a positive outcome; suffering a defeat and learning nothing is inexcusable. Make the most of the educational opportunity. Why did this occur? Were contingency plans utilized? Were primary and contingency plans well-thought out? Were you pleased with the response of your personnel? Did they respond as a team? Identify individuals who performed poorly, failing to rise to the occasion. Identify those who exhibited leadership skills and achieved beyond expectations. Who brought important subject matter expertise to the table?

Involve others in pursuit of solutions so they can feel the tangible benefits of fighting back and not giving up. This can be an opportunity for building the character of the people around you, and building your own character and experience. Evaluate your own behavior and performance throughout the crisis; in hindsight, would you have made the same decisions, taken the same actions, said the same things? Will you be more poised and effective in future under similar circumstances? If you are disappointed with your performance, can you forgive yourself? It's important not to be too hard on yourself. You are human and should also be given an opportunity to learn and improve. In most cases, you will be far more critical of yourself than anyone else.

Sometimes the punches just keep coming. An example is continuous defection by clients. Even those among us with the coldest blood wear down in the face of such a sequence of setbacks. Don't be a static target. Communicate with the clients and gain an understanding of their perspective. Why are they leaving your company? What would it take to win them back? You can't just cover your head with your arms and wait for the onslaught to end. You, more than anyone else, must be able to see clearly and decide how, or when, to change direction. Figure out how to make a few changes that alter the playing field. This may buy you time needed to identify and implement more changes that will ultimately help you to stabilize the situation.

PART FIVE
WHEN THE TURNAROUND
TAKES HOLD

CHAPTER 11
Maintain Positive Momentum

Previous chapters dealt with the decisions you must make, and actions you must undertake, to achieve the turnaround. In this chapter attention is focused on what you should do to maintain and build on the firm's favorable trajectory, in order to ensure its ongoing prosperity.

Following all the stress and hard work of the turnaround, it's natural for everyone in the firm to relax and admire the achievement. Undoubtedly, kudos are well deserved, and you should recognize those who've earned the praise. However, the most important priority as the firm returns to health is to remain focused. The last thing you want to allow is a regression to the bad old days.

To keep people focused, engaged, and motivated, adhere to four messages:

- Maintain a sense of urgency,

- Raise the bar,

- Invest in people, and

- Hold your strategy.

Maintain a Sense of Urgency

With the existential (bankruptcy) threat removed, the concern that the firm will fail if people don't pull together becomes much more remote. As you attempt to keep everyone focused, you may well find that one of your most important allies in the early days of the turnaround—a sense of fear—is no longer available to motivate the staff.

You must continuously remind your staff that your competitors are striving to get better each and every day. This means that if you are not all working intensely to get better as well, you are actually losing ground. A mild case of paranoia can actually be quite healthy.

While you don't want to create disabling or disruptive fear or anxiety, one of the ways to inject a sense of urgency into peoples' minds is by raising the bar, especially on mission-critical functions within the firm. Keeping people occupied with new tasks and challenges will reduce the likelihood they will become complacent.

Raise The Bar

A common mistake managers make is to gather the staff in a town hall setting, urge them to be focused, and then fail to provide the structure that creates the focus. Go beyond speeches, and fashion a setting that provides motivation and focus. Quality targets, efficiency benchmarks, client communication improvements, and disciplined Value Proposition processes are tangible things people can relate and adhere to. Coupling people's compensation to benchmarks and processes will properly align incentives.

Ensure existing products and services are of the highest quality. If you've instituted metrics for quality control, consider raising them. Your people may howl a bit, but they will eventually come to appreciate and take pride in the quality of their work. From a personal growth perspective, it's important for staff, especially middle managers, to learn that quality can *always* be improved further.

After a period of growth, it's appropriate to seek new efficiencies through cost-cutting. But make sure you are not turning the entire firm (and yourself) into cost-cutters as opposed to efficiency-seekers. The difference is that the former only cut: the latter cut and seek to invest the savings wisely to support future growth.

Continue to look for process improvements, taking into account client feedback. Encourage staff to participate, identifying areas for improvement; offer incentives for outstanding contributions. Not only does this harness everyone to a common cause, it also reduces the risk that staff will feel excluded from the decision-making process. You must avoid leaving the staff feeling that management rules by decree, without seeking opinions from a broader base. Participation will get everyone involved and enthusiastic.

Revisit all the processes deemed "good enough" in the early days, and seek to make them better.

If you've concluded that you made mistakes in the past (and an honest answer to this question is "Yes!"), now is a good time to revisit and amend the earlier decisions. This may not always be a viable option, but the effort should be made if at all possible.

Where appropriate, you may want to revisit and renegotiate contracts with external parties, this time from a position of greater strength. The point is not to take unfair advantage of partners, clients, and suppliers, but rather to neutralize situations in which you were being taken advantage of. As you seek to do this, you must be certain that you are, in fact, being fair. There is a strong likelihood that some staff members will urge you to take negotiating positions that are more advantageous to them personally than to the firm. Be on the lookout for these manipulators. Evaluate your positions from every angle, to be certain, on each occasion, that you are moving toward fairness—not creating an unfair situation for the counterparty.

The firm's clients are among its most important assets. Clients provide the revenue that makes doing business worthwhile, and they can also be a critical source of feedback about your offerings, the marketplace, and the competition. In order to take advantage of the collective wisdom of your clients, you must be seen as a trusted partner. In order to be seen as a partner rather than merely as a vendor, you must show loyalty to your clients, by consistently providing excellent service. Too many firms forget about loyalty to customers when it's no longer convenient, especially when they no longer feel under the existential threat of bankruptcy. This is a very short-term view, and as seen in earlier sections, can be a cause of distress.

The upshot is that you must create direct and open lines of communication with your clients. Communication should flow in both directions: from your firm to the client, and feedback from the client back to your firm. Once you have the client feedback mechanism in place, your clients will be the best source of information for future product and service ideas.

The intimate exchange of information will also help you to learn more about your client, the marketplace, and your competitors. The knowledge that the market is shifting significantly, or that a competitor is getting more aggressive, can serve as a powerful motivating force.

With more resources and cash on hand, it's natural to become less disciplined in the funding of new product ideas. Resist this urge. Ensure every new offering has a defensible Value Proposition. As highlighted in an earlier section, often the best place to vet the viability of ideas is to seek feedback from existing clients. Establishing and maintaining close relationships with clients will make them far more willing to share their wisdom. As before, you will document their opinions, but not follow them blindly.

Continue to Invest in People

Exhibiting loyalty to your staff is a good way to motivate people. Reward them for persevering through the hardships of the turnaround period. This does not mean you should splurge without limit or restraint, but it's important to reward sacrifices by rolling back austerity measures, addressing compensation, promotion, growth and learning opportunities. As you reward the staff, do keep in mind that expectations continue to be formed. Any rewards provided now will be expected in future. So, be fair, but don't go overboard.

Give people opportunities to switch jobs and departments. This keeps the staff engaged and stimulated. It also proves your commitment to their human capital development, and builds up the firm's bench with much greater depth. The diverse experiences will be especially useful for your talented managers, who will gain a much broader understanding and appreciation for the firm's various working parts.

Continue the ongoing process of talent assessment within the firm. Now that there is more cash on hand, you may want to revisit earlier staffing decisions. The cash can be used to provide fair and dignified separation packages in the event you feel additional personnel must be let go.

Think Strategically and Don't Overreach

With bankruptcy fears subsiding, your attention must quickly swing from short-term decisions to strategic, longer-term considerations. Now is the time to chart the firm's future course. Ironically, many companies run into trouble because they are unprepared for success. Here are a number of actions to undertake in preparation for future growth:

- Line up additional manufacturing capacity, quality assurance, sales and support staff, and beef up the human resources department, as necessary.

- Maintain the culture that is working.

- Look for the competition's weaknesses and seek to exploit them.

- Continue to examine your own weaknesses and seek to correct them.

- Look for global opportunities and seek distribution partners who can expand your reach to new client bases.

- Continue to invest in R&D to ensure future income streams.

The items listed above are those you must proactively undertake. Below are some actions you must avoid:

- Do not initiate too many—10 may be too many—new projects. New product ideas need to make sense and be practical, based on where you want the firm to go.

- Some new ideas may cannibalize existing products. Is the expected upside from the new products worth the risk to existing income streams?

- Avoid being pulled into non-core areas beyond the management team's capabilities.

- If strategic considerations call for such expansion, first add the appropriate expertise to the management team.

- Be clear about what the new products will do for the clients and how they will add value to the offerings.

- Avoid growing too fast: doing so can force you to overextend resources and hire lesser candidates you would otherwise not consider if you didn't have to feed the growth monster.

Finally, do not allow others to place your unit on a pedestal; do not allow expectations to grow out of control.

It's a long way down off that pedestal: if you start believing in your own manifest destiny, and forget that everything takes hard work, you'll be feeding unrealistic expectations, and setting everyone up for disappointment. Modesty is far more becoming, and it's much easier to operate under the radar, rather than create a clear target for competitors to zero in on.

With some success, you may be tempted to bet big on something. On the one hand, it's important to remain patient and selective. On the other hand, you still want to be bold if the opportunity arises. Initiatives or deals you may be tempted to undertake include: acquisitions, partial or complete sale of the company, or a move to a new distributor or supplier.

Acquisitions: Purchasing another entity, or being acquired by another, can be a "high-risk high-reward" proposition.

Several excellent books have been written on the subject; here are a few observations for your consideration:

One of the main challenges you'll encounter as you attempt to acquire another firm will be a lack of transparency—unwillingness or inability on the target institution's part to share important factual information about its finances, true successes, and failures.

The need for transparency also applies to the firm's owner-managers: do they intend to stick around post-acquisition and apply themselves and their unique skills to make the combined entity a success, or are they only interested in taking their money and departing as soon as possible?

If they are intending to "take the money and run," it may be because they have other interests to pursue, or are just tired. But, it may be due to their perception the company they have sold you is a lemon. In either case, once they've headed off into the sunset (with your money in their bank accounts), you may be left with an empty and relatively useless shell.

Acquisition talk can take on a life of its own. Once a certain, critical mass of signals about acquisition have been relayed, it's near-impossible to bail out, even if you begin to have doubts about the deal. Don't place yourself in such a situation.

Partial or Complete Sale of Own Company: The decision to be owned by another company may *seem* to offer low risk. After all, your firm's investors (possibly including yourself as a shareholder) will be getting paid, and you have the advantage of knowing how much your firm is worth before you agree to a price.

Before you take any action, try to gain an understanding of the acquirer's true intentions. Will your firm be broken up and redistributed among the acquirer's assets? Will it operate more independently, retaining much of its own form and culture? More personally, what will happen to existing management, including you? If you sell only a partial stake, what is the exit strategy? That is, does your firm retain the right to buy back its shares if the acquirer fails to buy out the entire firm from you over a certain number of years? Can you subsequently engage in discussions with other suitors, or will restrictions apply?

Keep in mind that suitors are looking at your firm because they believe there is money to be made on your sustained growth, or on growth your technology or services can help them realize elsewhere. Don't sell the firm short. In other words, once you fully understand the value the acquirer sees in you, ensure the offer price is commensurate with expected returns. Going a step further, ask yourself whether your firm can realize this additional growth on its own. That is, without a new parent. Perhaps you can take the firm to new heights and sell it at a later date for much more?

Move to New Distributors or Suppliers: Once you've become more successful, big-name distributors or suppliers may begin to court you. While flattering, be wary of exclusivity requirements imposed by such partners. Will they require you to deal with them exclusively? If so, you would be putting all your eggs in one basket. What will happen if the new partner suddenly reneges? Would you be able to reconstruct your supply or distribution networks? Do you believe the partners will give you the proper priority? Do your existing supplier(s) do a good enough job?

Whether you are contemplating an acquisition, sale or new partnership arrangement, you must ask yourself:

- What do you realistically stand to gain from the move?

- What are the downsides?

- How much certainty is there of a positive outcome?

- Is there an exit strategy if you choose to reverse your decision?

The best way to protect your firm from a disappointing (and embarrassing) outcome is to learn enough about the prospective acquisition target, parent, or partner. Ideally, you could apply all the lessons of this book to learn about the counterparty's operations and staff. This will help you to gauge the fit and advisability of the deal, and gauge the correct price for the transaction.

In general, however, very comprehensive due diligence can be intellectually challenging and time-consuming. Invariably, the counterparty will want to give you the least amount of information needed to achieve the deal. There may also be situations in which some of the other party's owners are in favor of the deal while others are not; you may find yourself on the sidelines as they battle it out on their way to a decision. Competitors may also sense the upcoming action and step in to thwart your efforts. This can create an acute sense of urgency that makes it difficult or impossible to spend the amount of time you would want to invest in comprehensive due diligence.

Always keep in mind that any deal must fit your firm's strategy—don't get dragged into someone else's strategy.

AFTERWORD

Leadership guru John C. Maxwell said, "Everything rises and falls on Leadership."

Turning around a firm is not rocket science but, in line with Maxwell's comment, it does require strong leadership. To be successful, you must understand basic business principles, and possess the presence, confidence, and emotional strength to lead and manage people in pursuit of a common cause.

Gaining or further developing the necessary skills and awareness described herein will serve you well throughout your working life. The significant demand for such abilities will ensure you enjoy a lucrative career. In addition, you will find that there is great satisfaction in building a successful enterprise, and watching your employees grow and stretch their wings. Helping people realize their potential and chase their dreams more effectively will give you a strong sense of personal accomplishment.

Turning a distressed company around is a big challenge—one which shouldn't be accepted lightly, and one which will surely stretch you to your limits. There will be low moments, but the rewards for all concerned are well worth the effort. Your commitment and belief in the ultimate outcome is crucial to success.

Good luck.

REFERENCES

Emotional Intelligence & People Skills

Bolton, Robert. *People Skills: How to Assert Yourself, Listen to Others, and Resolve Conflicts*. New York: Simon and Schuster, Inc., 1979.

Dimitrius, Jo-Ellan, and Mazzarella, Mark. *Reading People: How to Understand People and Predict Their Behavior–Anytime, Anyplace*. New York: The Ballantine Publishing Group, 1999.

Goleman, Daniel. *Emotional Intelligence: Why It Can Matter More Than IQ*. New York: Bantam, 2005.

Goleman, Daniel. *Working with Emotional Intelligence*. New York: Bantam, 2000.

Tavris, Carol. *Anger, the Misunderstood Emotion*. New York: Touchstone, 1989.

Know Your Business

Charan, Ram. *Profitable Growth is Everyone's Business: 10 Tools You Can Use Monday Morning.* New York: Crown Business, 2004.

Garvin, David A., and Roberto, Michael A. "Change Through Persuasion." *Harvard Business Review*, February, 2005.

Light, Paul C. *The Four Pillars of High Performance: How Robust Organizations Achieve Extraordinary Results.* New York: McGraw-Hill, 2005.

Globalization

Friedman, Thomas L. *The World is Flat: A Brief History of the Twenty-First Century.* New York: Farrar, Straus, and Giroux, 2005.

Govindarajan, Vijay and Gupta, Anil K. *The Quest for Global Dominance: Transforming Global Presence into Global Competitive Advantage.* San Francisco: Jossey Bass, 2001.

Strategy & Winning

Diamond, Jared. *Guns, Germs, and Steel: The Fates of Human Societies.* New York: W. W. Norton & Co., 1997.

Dick, Frank. *Winning: Motivation for Business, Sport & Life.* London: Abingdon Publishing, 1997.

Santamaria, Jason A., Martino, Vincent, and Clemons, Eric K. *The Marine Corps Way.* New York: McGraw-Hill, 2004.

Sun Tzu (translated by Ralph D. Sawyer). *The Art of War.* Boulder: Westview Press, 1994.

Leadership

Goleman, Daniel. "Leadership That Gets Results." *Harvard Business Review*, March-April 2000, pp. 78-90.

Machiavelli, Niccolo (translated by W. K. Marriott). *The Prince*. The Project Gutenberg EBook of The Prince. www.gutenberg.org.

Maxwell, John C. *The 21 Irrefutable Laws of Leadership*. Nashville: Nelson Business, 1998.

Welch, Jack, with Byrne, John A. *Jack: Straight From the Gut*. New York: Warner Business Books, 2001

Recruiting, Hiring and Firing

Cohn, Jeffrey M., Khurana, Rakesh, and Reeves, Laura. "Growing Talent as if Your Business Depended on It." *Harvard Business Review*, October 2005, pp. 1-7.

Smart, Bradford D. *Topgrading: How Leading Companies Win by Hiring, Coaching, and Keeping the Best People*. New York: Portfolio Hardcover, 2005.

INDEX

About the Author

The author is the founder and president of The Light Brigade Corporation, which provides leadership and risk management advisory services to corporations, educational institutions, and government agencies. Prior to founding The Light Brigade, the author held senior strategy, client service, and product management positions at a number of public and private corporations. Dr. Bar-Or has lectured extensively in academic and professional settings on the subjects of risk management and leadership best practices. He holds a Ph.D. and M.A. in finance from the Wharton School of the University of Pennsylvania, as well as an M.A. and B.A. (*summa cum laude*) in economics, and a bachelor of engineering degree from Canada's McMaster University.

Contacting Yuval Bar-Or

Yuval Bar-Or is the founder and president of the Light Brigade Corporation, which owns and administers several websites:

www.respectrisk.com – an educational resource on Risk, Risk-taking, and Risk Mitigation.

www.leadershiprisk.com – a site dedicated to Leadership, Leadership Risk, and Leadership Development.

www.creditsolutionsdemystified.com – a site dedicated to credit risk management solutions; catering to an international clientele primarily in the financial services industry.

Yuval Bar-Or may be reached through the **Contact Us** screen of any of these websites.

Is a PhD for Me?

Life in the Ivory Towers: a Cautionary Guide for Doctoral Students

Yuval Bar-Or

<u>Available April 2009</u>

Printed in the United States
217196BV00004B/13/P